OBAMACARE SURVIVAL GUIDE

The Affordable Care Act and What It Means for You and Your Healthcare

Complied by

Bartholomew Okonkwo

OBAMACARE SURVIVAL GUIDE

Book Compilation Copyright ©2013 by Bartholomew C. Okonkwo

This book is a collection of random facts from all over the internet. Sources are almost always

official sources, not-for-profits and news organizations.

ISBN-13: 978-1481997874

CreateSpace Independent Publishing Platform

Third Edition: September 2013

CONTENTS

INTRODUCTION

False Assumptions on the Health Care Law

An ad from a conservative advocacy group attacks the federal health care law by asking misleading and loaded questions about its impact. The ad features a mother named Julie, who asks, "If we can't pick our own doctor, how do I know my family's going to get the care they need?" The law doesn't prohibit Julie from picking her own doctor.

She further assumes the government is going to be intimately involved in her family's health decisions in asking, "Can I really trust the folks in Washington with my family's health care?" Unless Julie's family becomes eligible for Medicaid under the law, she'll be getting private insurance, just as she is now (as best we can infer from the ad).

The TV spot, which Americans for Prosperity began, airing in Ohio and Virginia July 9, directs viewers to the website ObamacareRiskFactors.com, which is more misleading than the ad itself. The site warns of reduced wages and hours for those who work for small employers that aren't even subject to the law, for instance.

Ad Wars Resume

Over the past four years, the Affordable Care Act has been the focus of a hefty share of ad dollars. But those for and against aren't done arguing about it yet — in fact, the war is heating up as major provisions of the law are about to take effect. In October, the health insurance exchanges will start accepting customers, and in 2014, the individual mandate, requiring most Americans to have insurance or pay a fine, kicks in.

So while Julie, a mother of two, prods viewers to feed their doubts about the law, another mom praises the benefits of the legislation in a TV ad from Organizing for Action, a nonprofit group that advocates for the president's policies. In that spot, airing on cable channels CNN, MSNBC, Bravo and Lifetime, Stacey Lihn says the law eliminated lifetime caps on coverage. True, lifetime limits were prohibited early on, in 2010, and annual limits completely phase out on Jan. 1, 2014. Lihn, who spoke at the Democratic National Convention and has documented her family's story on her personal blog, says that her daughter, Zoe, who was born with a congenital heart defect, "was halfway to her cap before her first birthday. Thanks to Obamacare, we can now afford the care that Zoe needs."

The conservative ad is more general, and we don't know much about the circumstances of the family in it. The mother, Julie, says her son had seizures two years ago and she has questions about Obamacare. Julie asks, "If we can't pick our own doctor, how do I know my family's going to get the care they need?"

But Julie doesn't mean that she won't be able to actually select a physician on her own, as the question implies. Instead, the worry is that she won't be able to keep her current doctor.

AFP spokesman Levi Russell told us that the law will limit provider networks and the choice of doctors for "millions" of Americans. But the support for that claim mainly pertains to those who would be buying their own insurance on new insurance exchanges or new Medicaid enrollees who will qualify for the program under the law's Medicaid expansion. And most of those individuals will be newly insured.

We can infer from the ad that Julie's family has insurance and wouldn't be seeking it on the exchanges or Medicaid. But we don't know for sure. Russell would not provide more information on Julie's circumstances other than to say she and her family are real, not actors. He said the group didn't want to make Julie's family the "centerpiece" of the ad campaign. "Instead, their experience should point others to go learn more for themselves and how they personally will be impacted," he said.

Let's assume Julie's family has employer-sponsored insurance, as 57 percent of non-elderly Americans do. AFP points out that the nonpartisan Congressional Budget Office has estimated that those with work-based coverage will decline by 7 million, on net, because of the law by 2023.

That figure is a combination of workers losing coverage, others gaining it and others buying insurance elsewhere. The CBO estimated that for 2019 — when the net figure is 8 million — those losing an offer of employer-based insurance, which they would have received had the law not been enacted, would be 12 million, with 7 million others gaining work-based coverage because of the law, and 3 million more declining their employers' offer and getting insurance elsewhere. CBO has explained in its previous estimates that businesses dropping coverage are likely to be smaller companies with low-income workers who would be able to get subsidies to buy insurance on the exchanges.

It's possible Julie will find herself among the employees who lose coverage, buy a new plan elsewhere and not have her same doctor in the provider network. But her chances are small: 160 million Americans are expected to have work-based coverage in 2023 under the law, up from 155 million in 2013.

AFP provided two other pieces of support for this claim. A March 1, 2013, *Wall Street Journal* article said that some insurance plans sold on exchanges will likely have small networks of providers in order to keep premium costs down: The insurers were asking for a discount from hospital groups in exchange for the hospitals getting new customers as part of a small network. And a Health Affairs study found 31 percent of doctors didn't accept new Medicaid patients in 2011. That's not due to the health care law, but it's a concern since the law will expand Medicaid eligibility by about 12 million in the coming decade. That study also said an increase in fees to primary care physicians under the law — for 2013 and 2014 — could boost the acceptance rate, at least temporarily. But doctors not being open to new patients are a problem generally: Eighteen percent weren't accepting new privately insured patients.

Perhaps more germane to this losing-your-doctor worry is the fact that the Affordable Care Act doesn't guarantee — and simply can't — that everyone who likes their doctor and their current health plan can keep them, as President Obama has often claimed. As we've said before, employers are free to switch or drop insurance plans under the law — just as they were before it was enacted. And workers who change jobs have no guarantee — before or after the law — that their new health plan will include their doctors in provider networks.

Premiums, Pay Checks and Big Government

Julie goes on to ask, "What am I getting in exchange for higher premiums and a smaller paycheck?" Again, we don't know Julie's circumstances and why she assumes her paycheck is going to get smaller and her premiums are going up. But it's true that expanded benefits required by the law have caused premiums for work-based plans to go up, on average.

7

When family premiums for employer plans jumped 9 percent from 2010 to 2011, experts told us the Affordable Care Act was responsible for a 1 percent to 3 percent hike, with the remainder due to higher medical costs, the usual culprit for increasing premiums. The law's provisions that caused the bump were the elimination of preexisting condition exclusions for children, the requirement that dependents be covered on their parents' plan to age 26, free coverage of preventive care, and the increase in caps on annual coverage.

So those are some of the increased benefits that Julie is already getting in exchange for slightly higher premiums.

For 2012, employer-based insurance went up a much smaller 4 percent on average. The growth in national health spending from 2009 to 2011 has been at historic lows, around 4 percent, and that trend is expected to continue for 2012 and 2013. Experts mainly say the down economy is the reason for reduced growth in spending, though it's possible the Affordable Care Act's emphasis on new payment models may be leading to more efficient care by health care providers.

If Julie purchases her own insurance, it's unknown what exactly would happen to her premium, as we've explained before. Some individuals will pay more, and some will pay less. Some will get significantly more generous benefits for higher premiums; others may not even want a more generous plan. Benefits and premiums vary widely on that market, and the change in premiums for individuals will likely also vary widely — depending on what benefits they have now, health status, the protections of the state they live in and more. The Affordable Care Act does prevent discrimination based on preexisting conditions, limit variation in premium rates (to age, where you live, family size and tobacco use), and require a minimum benefit standard for these plans.

Most of those purchasing plans on the exchanges — about 80 percent — will qualify for government subsidies to offset the premium cost, according to the Congressional Budget Office. If Julie's family earns up to 400 percent of the federal poverty level — $94,200 for a family of four — the family will qualify for a subsidy.

Finally, Julie wonders how well the government can manage her health care, asking, "Can I really trust the folks in Washington with my family's health care?" But the law doesn't put the government in charge of health care decisions — despite the many claims we've seen over the years to the contrary. This isn't a "government-run" plan or "takeover," as so many have tried to claim. There's no board deciding who gets brain surgery or picking anybody's doctor for them.

The law greatly expands private insurance, bringing millions of new customers to insurance companies. It's true there are new insurance regulations as we've mentioned — no annual or lifetime limits on coverage, no preexisting condition exclusions, a standard set of minimum benefit requirements for plans on the exchanges. But those are consumer protections, not rules that put Washington in charge of managing families' health care.

More Questions than Answers

The AFP ad encourages viewers to visit ObamacareRiskFactors.com, where they can input some basic information about themselves and answer the question, "Are you at risk under the new healthcare law?" But don't expect an unbiased answer.

When we said we worked for an employer with 0 to 50 employees, our first risk factor was a warning that our hours or pay could be cut because of "requirements to provide insurance to all employees."

The warning said that "government forces employers to make a difficult choice: reduce employee's hours or wages or go out of business." But employers with less than 50 full-time workers aren't subject to any requirement to provide insurance to their employees. There was no mention of that, despite the fact that we had said we worked for a small employer. (The administration recently announced that it was delaying the requirement for employers with 50 or more workers for one year, until 2015.)

The risk factors we received also warned of "longer lines and delayed care," citing a doctor shortage of 45,000 primary care physicians by 2020, estimated by the Association of American Medical Colleges. The warning doesn't make clear that the AAMC said a shortage was predicted before the law was passed, but the shortage coupled with adding tens of millions to the rolls of the insured is certainly a legitimate concern. AAMC said the coverage expansion will "exacerbate a physician shortage driven by the rapid expansion of the number of Americans over age 65." It called for Medicare-funded residency training to help alleviate the problem.

AFP exaggerates by saying that "[t]hese problems will continue to get worse as one-third of doctors will retire over the next decade — many fueled by ObamaCare's rules and regulations." AAMC says simply that one-third will retire because "[o]ur doctors are getting older, too."

Americans for Prosperity almost gets it right when it says that "ObamaCare mandates that employers provide insurance coverage to all full-time employees, but it doesn't mandate that coverage be provided for spouses or children." The law does mandate that insurance policies cover children up to age 26. But it's true there's no mandate for coverage of spouses.

Of course, there was no mandate for employers to cover spouses before the law, and some firms have charged more for spouses or, for a small percentage of large firms, excluded them from coverage. The human resources consulting firm Mercer has said that its 2012 health benefits survey found 4 percent of employers with 5,000 or more employees denied coverage for spouses. MarketWatch reported in a February 2013 article that the practice, primarily used for spouses who could get insurance through their own jobs, could increase as health care expenses continue to rise (with or without the Affordable Care Act) and as the state-based exchanges created under the law give spouses another option for coverage. MarketWatch quoted Joan Smyth, a benefits consultant at Mercer as saying, "When there's a place for people to go, employers won't feel as beholden or compelled to cover the spouse."

It remains to be seen whether the lack of a spouse mandate will have an impact.

The risk factors also warned that "[f]ailing to purchase insurance will result in a tax penalty of $695." True, when the law is fully implemented in 2016. But the AFP site only tells half the story. It doesn't ask whether individuals already have insurance or not, and it says nothing about opportunities for federal subsidies to help the uninsured buy coverage or expansion of Medicaid eligibility.

We're not suggesting that the Affordable Care Act shouldn't prompt questions and concern from Americans. There are many unknowns about how exactly a law of this magnitude will play out, particularly its impact on those who buy their own insurance. But don't expect honest answers from a partisan anti-Obamacare campaign.

Sources: www.factcheck.org

CHAPTER ONE

Understating the Health Care Reform

The health care reform debate in the United States has been a political issue for many years, focusing upon increasing coverage, decreasing the cost and social burden of healthcare, insurance reform, and the philosophy of its provision, funding, and government involvement. In the United States healthcare has always been a private industry. Citizens who can afford it purchase insurance and are thus provided healthcare. However there have been some big issues with this system, these include unfair and unjustified rate hikes, limited coverage and denial of health care based off of pre-existing conditions.

There is significant debate regarding the quality of the U.S. healthcare system relative to those of other countries. Physicians for a National Health Program, a political advocacy group, have claimed that a free market solution to health care provides a lower quality of care, with higher mortality rates, than publicly funded systems. The quality of health maintenance organizations and managed care has also been criticized by this same group.

According to a 2000 study of the World Health Organization, publicly funded systems of industrial nations spend less on health care, both as a percentage of their GDP and per capita, and enjoy superior population-based health care outcomes. However, conservative commentator David Gratzer and the Cato Institute, a libertarian think tank, have both criticized the WHO's comparison method for being biased; the WHO study marked down countries for having private or fee-paying health treatment and rated countries by comparison to their expected health care performance, rather than objectively comparing quality of care.

Some medical researchers say that patient satisfaction surveys are a poor way to evaluate medical care. Researchers at the RAND Corporation and the Department of Veterans Affairs asked 236 elderly patients in two different managed care plans to rate their care, then examined care in medical records, as reported in Annals of Internal Medicine. There was no correlation. "Patient ratings of health care are easy to obtain and report, but do not accurately measure the technical quality of medical care," said John T. Chang, UCLA, lead author.

There are health losses from insufficient health insurance. A 2009 Harvard study published in the American Journal of Public Health found more than 44,800 excess deaths annually in the United States due to Americans lacking health insurance. More broadly, estimates of the total number of people in the United States, whether insured or uninsured, who die because of lack of medical care were estimated in a 1997 analysis to be nearly 100,000 per year.

In the meantime, the US continues to be the country with the highest proportion of uninsured people in the developed world. An estimated 50 million Americans are uninsured and another 25 million are underinsured, meaning they can't pay the difference between what their insurance will cover and the total cost of their medical bills. Someone files for bankruptcy every 30 seconds in the US because of a serious health problem, according to a Harvard University study. Further, an estimated 77 million Baby Boomers are reaching retirement age, which combined with significant annual increases in healthcare costs per person will place enormous budgetary strain on U.S. state and federal governments. Maintaining the long-term fiscal health of the U.S. federal government is significantly dependent on healthcare costs being controlled.

Democratic politicians proudly point to the Patient Protection and Affordable Care Act, the bill that was signed by President Obama in March 2010, as real progress, but Physicians for a National Health Program (PNHP), an organisation of doctors who support healthcare for all, say the bill is nothing more than a false promise of reform.

Instead of eliminating the real problem, the new legislation will enrich and further entrench the profit-driven, private health insurance industry, and will still leave 30 million without coverage in 2019, according to the CBO. As IBD reported, that figure could be much higher if the law causes premiums to spike and encourages people to drop coverage despite the law's mandate.

If Republicans however, have their way, the 45 million seniors and people with disabilities who rely on Medicare will see their out-of-pocket costs double - or do without treatment altogether. Maybe there's a campaign slogan here: Health-care costs will make you sick—but they'd kill you without Obamacare.

The Need for Reform

The United States spends a higher proportion of its GDP on health care (19.3% in ref cited, but now 16%, lagging other rich countries) than any other country in the world, except for East Timor (Timor-Leste). In 2009, the U.S. had the highest healthcare costs relative to the size of the economy (GDP) in the world, with an estimated 50.2 million citizens (approximately 15.6% of the September 2011 estimated population of 312 million) without insurance coverage. The number of employers who offer health insurance is declining. Costs for employer-paid health insurance are rising rapidly: since 2001, premiums for family coverage have increased 78%, while wages have risen 19% and prices have risen 17%, according to a 2007 study by the Kaiser Family Foundation.

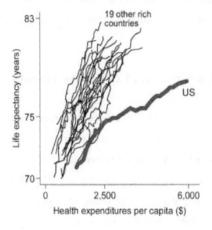

Life expectancy compared to healthcare spending from 1970 to 2008, in the US and the next 19 most wealthy countries by total GDP.

But even though US citizens pay more for healthcare, they get less of it, resulting in a lowly 37th place ranking among healthcare systems in the world, according to a study by the World Health Organization based on quality and fairness. In terms of the infant mortality rate, a common marker for the overall state of healthcare systems, the US was outranked by all of the following countries according to the CIA's World Factbook: Sweden (3rd), Japan (4th), France (7th), Norway (10th), Germany (14th), Israel (17th), Denmark (21st), United Kingdom (31st), Canada (35th), Taiwan (39th), Italy (41st) and even a few underdeveloped countries, including Cuba (43rd).

How can this paradox of the US spending the most and getting the least for its healthcare occur in the country with the world's largest economic output?

Claudia Schaufan, an Argentine physician and professor of comparative health policies at the University of California in Santa Cruz, explains that the common characteristics of healthcare systems in the developed world have to do with the universality of coverage and the lack of for-profit entities.

The key behind each of these systems is that they all outperform the US in terms of their infant mortality rates, administrative costs, the extent of population with coverage and the proportion of GDP spent on healthcare.

Furthermore, there are no documented instances of citizens going bankrupt because of medical care in these systems while, conversely, some studies have shown as many as 700,000 Americans suffer that fate annually.

Fixing the Problem: The Affordable Care Act Legislative History

Health care reform was a major topic of discussion during the 2008 Democratic presidential primaries. As the race narrowed, attention focused on the plans presented by the two leading candidates, New York Senator Hillary Clinton and the eventual nominee, Illinois Senator Barack Obama. Each candidate proposed a plan to cover the approximately 45 million Americans estimated to be without health insurance at some point during each year. One point of difference between the plans was that Clinton's plan was to require all Americans to obtain coverage (in effect, an individual health insurance mandate), while Obama's was to provide a subsidy but not create a direct requirement.

During the general election campaign between Obama and the Republican nominee, Arizona Senator John McCain, Obama said that fixing health care would be one of his four priorities if he won the presidency. After his inauguration, Obama announced to a joint session of Congress in February 2009 that he would begin working with Congress to construct a plan for health care reform. On March 5, 2009, Obama formally began the reform process and held a conference with industry leaders to discuss reform and requested reform be enacted before the Congressional summer recess; but the reform was not passed by the requested date. In July 2009, a series of bills were approved by committees within the House of

Representatives. Beginning June 17, 2009, and extending through September 14, 2009, three Democratic and three Republican Senate Finance Committee Members met for a series of 31 meetings to discuss the development of a health care reform bill. Over the course of the next three months, this group, Senators Max Baucus (D-Montana), Chuck Grassley (R-Iowa), Kent Conrad (D-North Dakota), Olympia Snowe (R-Maine), Jeff Bingaman (D-New Mexico), and Mike Enzi (R-Wyoming), met for more than 60 hours, and the principles that they discussed became the foundation of the Senate's health care reform bill. The meetings were held in public and broadcast by C-SPAN and can be seen on the C-SPAN web site or at the Committee's own web site. During the August 2009 congressional recess, many members went back to their districts and entertained town hall meetings to solicit public opinion on the proposals. During the summer recess, the Tea Party movement organized protests and many conservative groups and individuals targeted congressional town hall meetings to voice their opposition to the proposed reform bills.

President Obama delivered a speech to a joint session of Congress supporting reform and again outlining his proposals. His plan mentions: deficit neutrality; not allowing insurance companies to discriminate based on pre-existing conditions; capping out of pocket expenses; creation of an insurance exchange for individuals and small businesses; tax credits for individuals and small companies; independent commissions to identify fraud, waste and abuse; and malpractice reform projects, among other topics.

OMB Director Peter Orszag described aspects of the Obama administration's strategy during an interview in November 2009: "In order to help contain [Medicare and Medicaid] cost growth over the long term, we need a new health care system that has digitized information... in which that information is used to assess what's working and what's not more intelligently, and in which we're paying for quality rather than quantity while also encouraging prevention and wellness." He also argued for bundling payments and accountable care organizations, which reward doctors for teamwork and patient outcomes.

On November 7, the House of Representatives passed the Affordable Health Care for America Act on a 220–215 vote and forwarded it to the Senate for passage. The Senate failed to take up debate on the House bill and instead took up H.R. 3590, a bill regarding housing tax breaks for service members. As the United States Constitution requires all revenue-related bills to originate in the House, the Senate took up this bill since it was first passed by the House as a revenue-related modification to the Internal Revenue Code. The bill was then used as the Senate's vehicle for their health care reform proposal, completely revising the content of the bill. The bill as amended incorporated elements of earlier proposals that had been reported favorably by the Senate Health and Finance committees.

Passage in the Senate was temporarily blocked by a filibuster threat by Nebraska Senator Ben Nelson, who sided with the Republican minority. Nelson's support for the bill was won after it was amended to offer a higher rate of Medicaid reimbursement for Nebraska. The compromise was derisively referred to as the "Cornhusker Kickback" (and was later repealed by the reconciliation bill). On December 23, the Senate voted 60–39 to end debate on the bill, eliminating the possibility of a filibuster by opponents. The bill then passed by a vote of 60–39 on December 24, 2009, with all Democrats and two Independents voting for, and all Republicans voting against except one Republican senator (Jim Bunning, R-Ky.) not voting.

Although White House Chief of Staff Rahm Emanuel argued for a less ambitious bill, House Speaker Nancy Pelosi pushed back, dismissing Emanuel's scaled-down approach as "Kiddie Care". Obama's siding with comprehensive reform and the news that Anthem Blue Cross in California intended to raise premium rates for its patients by as much as 39% gave him a new line of argument for reform. Obama unveiled a health care reform plan of his own, drawing largely from the Senate bill. On February 22 he laid out a "Senate-leaning" proposal to consolidate the bills. On February 25, he held a meeting with leaders of both parties urging passage of a reform bill. The summit proved successful in shifting the political narrative away from the Massachusetts loss back to health care policy.

The most viable option for the proponents of comprehensive reform was for the House to abandon its own health reform bill, the Affordable Health Care for America Act, and to instead pass the Senate's bill, and then pass amendments to it with a different bill allowing the Senate to pass the amendments via the reconciliation process.

Initially, there were not enough supporters to pass the bill, thus requiring its proponents to negotiate with a group of pro-life Democrats, led by Congressman Bart Stupak. The group found the possibility of federal funding for abortion was substantive enough to cause their opposition to the bill. Instead of requesting inclusion of additional language specific to their abortion concerns in the bill, President Obama issued Executive Order 13535, reaffirming the principles in the Hyde Amendment. This concession won the support of Stupak and members of his group and assured passage of the bill.

The House passed the bill with a vote of 219 to 212 on March 21, 2010, with 34 Democrats and all 178 Republicans voting against it. The following day, Republicans introduced legislation to repeal the bill. They say that when the law is fully in effect, it will jeopardize the nation's fragile economic recovery. But Obama's allies say national health care could help strengthen the economy in part by encouraging health maintenance and prevention.

Obama signed the original bill into law on March 23, 2010. At the same time he also signed in the Health Care and Education Reconciliation Act, these Acts seek to overhaul the current healthcare system. By signing these Acts into law, "Obamacare" became the biggest overhaul to healthcare reform since Medicare / Medicaid which was signed into law in 1965. The law has been upheld by the Supreme Court.

Increasing Transparency, Protecting Consumers—What the Affordable Care Act Does

Fixing the system is a tall order as "Obamacare's" major coverage expansion takes effect on October 2013 and beyond. The U.S. is projected to spend $2.9 trillion on health care in 2013, approaching one of every five dollars in the economy, much more than any other advanced country. But Americans are not appreciably healthier and more than 48 million are uninsured. The nation's mix of private insurance and government programs supports many of the world's best hospitals, but overall the quality of care is uneven and much is wasted by lack of coordination and overtreatment, putting patients at risk. Fraud bleeds the system of tens of billions of dollars a year.

True insurance protects against catastrophic losses. Think of flood insurance covering the damage as the couch floats by the window, or a life insurance policy paying out after a loved one's death. Health insurance slants more toward maintenance care, such as annual checkups, that the other insurances tend to avoid. Good luck getting your car insurance to pick up your 60,000-mile tuneup.

The different types of insurance have had similar means of funding. Customers pay a fee set according to risk level. Screening guidelines kept out the riskiest individuals and mitigated the overall level of risk the company would assume. The excluded might have included homes in hurricane-prone areas or individuals with a history of serious health problems.

But the Affordable Care Act, or ACA, is changing how private health insurers can screen patients and the premiums they can charge. That change is causing a new health industry shift that could redefine its future. These are the biggies:

End to Pre-Existing Condition Discrimination: Insurance companies can no longer deny coverage to children because of a pre-existing condition like asthma and diabetes, providing peace of mind for parents of the more than 17.6 million children with pre-existing conditions. Starting in 2014, no American can be discriminated against due to a pre-existing condition.

Free Prevention Benefits: Some insurers will only pay for health care provided by a limited number or network of providers – including emergency health care. Others require prior approval before receiving emergency care at hospitals outside of their networks. This could mean financial hardship if you get sick or injured when you are away from home or not near a network hospital.

Insurers are now required to cover a number of recommended preventive services, such as cancer, diabetes and blood pressure screenings, without additional cost sharing such as copays or deductibles. The rules also set requirements on how health plans should reimburse out-of-network providers. This policy applies to all individual market and group health plans except those that are grandfathered.

Coverage for Young Adults: Under the law, most young adults who can't get coverage through their jobs can stay on their parents' plans until age 26 – a change that has already allowed 3.1 million young adults to get health coverage and given their families peace of mind.

End to Limits on Care: In the past, some people with cancer or other chronic illnesses ran out of insurance coverage because their health care expenses reached a dollar limit imposed by their insurance company. Under the health care law, insurers can no longer impose lifetime dollar limits on essential health benefits and annual limits are being phased out by 2014. More than 105 million Americans no longer have lifetime limits thanks to the new law.

End to Coverage Cancellations: Insurance companies can no longer drop your coverage when you get sick due to a mistake you made on your application.

Stopping Unreasonable Rate Increases: In every State and for the first time ever, insurance companies are required to publicly justify their actions if they want to raise rates by 10 percent or more. The Affordable Care Act prohibits some of the worst insurance industry practices that have kept affordable health coverage out of reach for millions of Americans. It provides families and individuals with new protections against discriminatory rates due to pre-existing conditions, holds insurance companies accountable for how they spend your premium dollars, and prevents insurance companies from raising your insurance premium rates without accountability or transparency.

Premium rebates if insurers underspend on care. The health law says that most insurers must spend at least 80 percent (85 percent for insurers covering large employers) of the premiums you pay on medical care and quality improvements. If insurers spend too much on overhead, such as salaries, bonuses, or administrative costs, as opposed to health care, they must issue premium rebates to consumers each summer.

Affordable Insurance Exchanges: Affordable Insurance Exchanges are one-stop marketplaces where consumers can choose a private health insurance plan that fits their health needs. Starting in 2014, they will offer to the public the same kinds of insurance choices members of Congress will have. Exchanges will select health plans qualified to offer coverage; facilitate consumer assistance, shopping and enrollment; and coordinate eligibility for the Exchange and potential premium assistance.

Guarantees Your Right to Appeal: You now have the right to ask that your plan reconsider its denial of payment for a service or treatment.

The Cons of Obamacare

The law has already expanded coverage of young adults by allowing them to stay on their parents' plans until they turn 26, outlawed lifetime limits on what insurance will cover, lowered the cost of drugs for seniors on Medicare, caused 13 million consumers to get premium rebates totalling some $1.1 billion, and expanded access to free preventive care for patients of all ages. But can it deliver its promise of affordable, quality coverage for millions more uninsured Americans without a cost spike that undermines benefits for others?

Costs will go up, not down, but how fast? If health care inflation remains at low or moderate levels, there should be room to bring in the uninsured. The law is an extremely polarizing issue, with its supporters and detractors seemingly equally passionate. What cannot be denied is the fact that the law does have several very serious potential problems:

*Government Rationing. Under Obamacare, choosing the ideal treatment for a particular condition will no longer be a decision made solely between a doctor and a patient. Instead, the government will be able to decide which treatments it considers to be "effective" in a particular situation, taking into consideration factors like a patient's age and health history. Although the program is theoretically supposed to limit health care costs, its long term effect will be to ration treatments to those the government feels deserve them.

*Economic Burden. The sheer scale of a health care program that includes every single adult United States citizen means that its cost will be massive. This cost will of necessity be passed along to the taxpayers, a drastic overall expense increase that could be particularly problematic in light of recent economic downturns. Individuals who have to spend more money on taxes will have less money to spend on consumer goods and services, which is the primary factor in improving the economy. Since more purchases from consumers mean more job availability, higher taxes due to Obamacare could well diminish any potential economic recovery.

*Mandated Coverage. The Obamacare program mandates that all United States citizens must get health insurance coverage. Anyone who does not get coverage will be forced to pay a fine in the form of an increased tax rate. This removes the freedom of choice from private citizens in regards to their personal finances and health decisions.

*Privacy Issues. If the government is to make decisions about what treatment and medications to provide for different individuals, it will need to maintain a staggering amount of personal information about those people's medical history, health conditions and other topics. This is information that once was confidential between a person and her doctor. Many individuals are very uncomfortable about the prospect of sharing every detail of their lives with the government, even if the government claims that it will not share this information with any other organizations.

*Wait Times. As was previously mentioned, it will likely become difficult to get some patients approved for expensive surgeries and other medical procedures. However, even people who do receive approval for these types of procedures will likely face extremely long wait times before actually receiving them due to the massive total expense of the program. This has already been seen in nations like Canada that have implemented similar programs.

* Doctor shortages. Obamacare expands government's role as the primary payer of health care by adding 18 million people to the Medicaid program, which on average reimburses doctors only 56 percent of the market rate for medical procedures. Due to increased regulation and less reimbursement, 66 percent of doctors are considering no longer accepting government health programs. Last summer, a study by the Association of American Medical Colleges found that the country will have 62,900 fewer doctors than its needs by 2015, thanks in large part to ObamaCare. At the same time, a survey of 13,000 doctors by the Physicians Foundation found that almost 60% of doctors say ObamaCare has made them less optimistic about the future of health care and they would retire today if they could.

*Universal Coverage Drawbacks. Since the Obamacare program mandates coverage for all citizens, and removes pre-existing condition exclusions, individuals who take very good care of themselves physically and are therefore in good health will wind up carrying the burden for people who may be obese, alcoholic, heavy smokers or who have made other poor health decisions. This type of universal program unintentionally punishes people who are healthy and rewards those who are unhealthy.

Who Wins With the New Legislation?

The most obvious winners appear to be the uninsured, people with preexisting conditions, people with expensive or chronic conditions, and small business owners. Some say the real winners are the pharmaceutical companies and the health insurers, who stand to gain 32 million more paying customers. Others say the economy is the winner, because more focus on prevention, early diagnosis, and treatment will reduce the burden of illness in this country and the percentage of the gross domestic product that goes toward health care costs.

Public reaction to these health care reforms has been mixed, with some polls showing majority support and others showing majority opposition. Many people will not feel the effects of the reforms until 2014, and their views may evolve over time as the law's benefits and drawbacks become more apparent. Public reaction to both the Social Security and

Medicare programs was also mixed when those laws were enacted—yet few people today want to see either program eliminated.

CHAPTER TWO

Health Insurance: Radical Changes Ahead

The Affordable Care Act (ACA) makes major changes to rules governing private health insurance in order to promote broader pooling of risk, prohibit discrimination on the basis of health status and pre-existing conditions, foster competition to enhance insurance market efficiency and affordability, promote prevention and wellness, and institute greater consumer protections. A series of proposed regulations (known as NPRMs) issued on November 26 outlined specifics for how many of these new rules would operate starting in 2014. In some cases, implementing the various goals of the ACA involve tradeoffs, which the proposed rules seek to balance.

Three proposed regulations were issued relating to

- Private insurance market reforms **http://www.gpo.gov/fdsys/pkg/FR-2012-11-26/pdf/2012-28428.pdf**
- Essential health benefits and actuarial value **http://www.gpo.gov/fdsys/pkg/FR-2012-11-26/pdf/2012-28362.pdf**
- Standards for wellness programs offered or required by employers who sponsor group health plans **http://www.gpo.gov/fdsys/pkg/FR-2012-11-26/pdf/2012-28361.pdf**

Market Reforms – This set of proposed rules govern the sale, pricing, and renewability of health insurance. These rules generally apply to the individual and small group health insurance markets, for coverage sold inside and outside of Exchanges. In general, these rules do not apply to so-called grandfathered health plans and policies. Key provisions in this proposed rule include:

1. Definition of group and individual health insurance markets - The definition would be based on the ultimate purchaser of health insurance – an individual or a small employer (defined in 2014 as a firm with at least two and up to 50 employees). This definition effectively changes the treatment of association coverage. Today, many individuals and small

23

businesses purchase coverage through associations – for example, through a local Chamber of Commerce or professional association, or some other membership organization. In many states, such associations are considered to be large groups, and so coverage sold through them today may be exempt from some or all of the rules that would otherwise apply to traditional health insurance markets for individuals and small employers. Under the market reform NPRM, associations that provide health insurance coverage for individuals and small employers would be subject to the same market rules that would otherwise apply to the individual and small group markets.

2. Guaranteed availability and renewability – The proposed rule would require insurers to accept all applicants for all individual and small group market policies, regardless of health status, occupation, or other risk factors. Only limited exceptions to this guaranteed issue requirement would apply:

- *Open enrollment periods for individual health insurance* – Small group issuers would be required to guarantee issue coverage year-round; but in the individual market, issuers could restrict the sale of policies to initial and annual open enrollment periods. At other times during the year, issuers would have to permit special enrollment opportunities of at least 30 days for individuals with qualifying events (such as a change in family or dependency status or the loss of eligibility for other coverage – similar to special enrollment rules that have applied to group health plans for many years).

- *Minimum participation and contribution rates* – As is true under federal law today, small group issuers would be allowed to require small employer plan sponsors to contribute a minimum amount toward participants' premiums and/or to enroll a minimum proportion of eligible employees.

- *Network or financial capacity limits* – Plans with a geographically distinct provider network issuers could also restrict the sale of coverage to individuals or small groups who reside outside of the plan's service area. Enrollment could also be limited by plans that can demonstrate they are at the limit of their network or financial capacity to serve new members. Also as current law requires, health insurance coverage would have to be renewable at the policyholder's discretion. Insurers would only be allowed to non-renew or discontinue coverage for nonpayment or late payment of premiums (the rule does not specify standards for late payment, such as requirements for notice or minimum grace periods), for an act of fraud by the policyholder, or for other limited reasons.

3. Premium rating and rate review – The proposed rule sets several new standards that would significantly change rating practices for individual and small group health insurance.

- *Single risk pool* – Insurers would be required to consider as a single risk pool the claims experience of all enrollees in all of its individual market health plans in a state. A similar rule would apply for small group market health insurers. As a result, premium differences across health plans offered by an issuer would reflect differences in benefits covered and would not vary based on health differences of the enrollees. This rule constitutes a significant change from current rating practices which can result in sicker people paying higher premiums than healthier people for similar benefits. This single risk pool requirement would apply to all plans offered by an insurer in a market, both inside and outside of an Exchange.

- *Modified community rating* – The proposed rule prohibits insurers from charging individuals or small groups differently based on pre-existing conditions, occupation, gender, duration of coverage, credit worthiness or most other factors. Premiums can only be adjusted based on certain factors, including:

- Family coverage – Premiums can vary based the number of adults and children in a family. States may establish uniform family tiers; otherwise, federal rules apply. Under these rules, a family's premium would be the sum of the individual premiums for each adult and each child (up to 3) under age 21 In other words, a family with two adults and three children under age 21 would not pay a higher premium if they had a fourth child. Individual premiums for children 21 and older covered under the policy are added without any limitation.

- Geography – Premiums can be adjusted for the geographic rating area in which the policy is sold. States may establish geographic rating areas, subject to federal standards and approval. The proposed rule requires rating areas must be of an adequate size (for example, no smaller than a metropolitan area) to support pooling of risk.

- Age – Premium adjustments are allowed based on age, up to a limit of three-to-one variation for adults age 21 to 64. The proposed rule would require the use of uniform, one-year age bands in the individual and small group markets. Among other things, use of a uniform age curve would simplify calculation of eligibility for premiums subsidies. (Under the ACA, premium tax credit subsidies are tied to the second lowest

25

cost silver plan in an Exchange. If insurers applied different age curves, there could be multiple second-lowest-cost silver-plans in an Exchange, depending on a person's age.) States may require narrower age bands or prohibit age adjustments altogether, as some do today.

- Tobacco use – The ACA permits premiums to vary based on tobacco use by a factor up to 1.5. Under the proposed rule – unlike uniform age bands – insurers would be given flexibility to determine how to make this adjustment within the overall limit. The proposed rule provides one permissible example – that insurers could apply a lower tobacco premium surcharge for younger individuals and a higher one for older individuals. Using the example in the proposed rule, a younger smoker might pay a few dollars more each month while the older smoker could be charged hundreds of dollars more each month. Importantly, under the ACA, premium tax credits do not apply to the tobacco surcharge, so it is possible the surcharge could render coverage unaffordable for older tobacco users. People who would have to pay more than 8 percent of family income for coverage are excused from the requirement to have health insurance because the cost is deemed unaffordable under the law.

Studies have shown that tobacco use tends to be higher among lower income individuals.3 The proposed rule does not define tobacco use (for example, what products or the frequency or regularity of tobacco use) and does not specify how insurers would collect and verify information about tobacco use, but requests comment on these questions. Tobacco rating is also permitted in the group market. Under the proposed rule, insurers would not be able to apply tobacco adjustments to small group rating unless tobacco users in the small group were also offered a wellness program that provides an opportunity to avoid paying the full surcharge. (see below) States may also limit further or prohibit tobacco rating adjustments.

- *Application of age and tobacco rating factors to group policies* – For groups, the proposed rule requires allowable rating factors (such as age, tobacco use) to be associated with specific employees and dependents. Issuers would be required to calculate per-member rates in order to develop a group premium. As for the amount employers would then contribute to coverage of each group member, the rule explicitly leaves to employers (of all sizes) flexibility to base their contribution either on the per member average, or on each group member's specific factors.

Essential Health Benefits and Actuarial Value – Another proposed rule relates to the content of private health insurance coverage, setting standards for covered benefits and cost sharing.

1. Essential Health Benefits – The ACA requires all non-grandfathered health plans in the individual and small group market, whether sold in or out of Exchanges, to cover essential health benefits (EHB). The ACA doesn't enumerate EHBs, but specifies 10 categories of EHBs that must be covered: a. Ambulatory patient services

b. Emergency services

c. Hospitalization

d. Maternity and newborn care

e. Mental health and substance use disorder services including behavioral health treatment

f. Prescription drugs

g. Rehabilitative and habilitative services and devices

h. Preventive and wellness services and chronic disease management

 i. Pediatric services, including vision and dental care

The proposed rule relies on benchmark plans to fill in the details of EHB, at least for 2014 and 2015. Under the proposed rule, states would be able to select a benchmark plan from a choice of ten popular (as measured by enrollment) private health plans today. These include the three largest small group health insurance products sold in a state, the three largest state employee health benefit plan options, the three largest federal employee health benefit plan options, or the largest commercial HMO plan sold in a state. If a state doesn't select a benchmark, the default choice will be the largest small group health plan. Any covered benefit under the benchmark plan would automatically be considered an essential health benefit. And any limits on the amount, scope, or duration of coverage under the benchmark plan would also be included in the definition of essential health benefits for that state (for example, if the benchmark plan limits rehabilitative therapies to 20 visits per year). However, separately, the ACA applies mental health parity rules to individual and small group health insurance policies.

In most states the benchmark plan would need to be supplemented because it lacks coverage for at least some EHB categories. For example, many existing private health plans today do not cover pediatric vision or dental benefits; many also do not cover habilitative services. The proposed rule specifies that supplementation is necessary if the benchmark plan does not cover any benefits in a category, and outlines a process for supplementation that generally relies on other benchmark plans.

Once the benchmark is established, issuers in a state must offer benefits that are substantially equal to the EHB benchmark plan. However, issuers have some flexibility to modify the EHB benchmark plan benefits. Under the proposed rule, within a category of EHB, issuers could substitute benefits or sets of benefits that are actuarially equivalent to those being replaced.4 Issuers that make such substitutions would be required to submit evidence of actuarial equivalence to the substituted benefits, to the state.

Separate rules apply to coverage for prescription drugs. For each therapeutic category or class of prescription drugs (for example, as defined by the United States Pharmacopeia or USP), health plans must cover the greater of one drug per class or category, or the same number of drugs per class or category as covered by the benchmark plan. Drugs in a class or category must be therapeutically distinct (for example, different doses of the same drug are counted as one drug, as are brand drugs and their generic equivalents.)

Some areas of ambiguity remain regarding how essential benefit rules will work in practice. For example, the proposed rule does not specify how services in the benchmark plan should be assigned to categories, within which insurers can modify and substitute benefits on an actuarially equivalent basis. Certain categories – such as "maternity and newborn care" – are quite specific and self-explanatory. However, others – such as ambulatory care – are broad and not well defined, leaving questions about which services are included. For instance, would home health or durable medical equipment best be categorized as ambulatory services or rehabilitative services? What category would apply to organ transplants? Also, some plans today cover expensive injectable drugs (such as chemotherapy drugs) as a medical service, not under their drug benefit. Would plans be able to continue to categorize chemotherapy in this way, and if so, follow substitution rules that apply for other medical benefits rather than apply the rules governing drug formularies? If so, plans may be able to apply restrictive limits to these medications. Finally, plans today vary in how they cover supplies used in the management of diabetes, which can easily cost thousands of dollars per year. Depending on the plan, blood glucose test strips and meters, syringes, and lancets may be covered as medical equipment and supplies, or under the prescription drug benefit, or under a separate disease management benefit, or just under broad category of ambulatory medical care and services. If insurers have flexibility to define the content of EHB categories in this way, the limitation on substitution only within categories would be less constraining.

The ACA applies two other general EHB standards to qualified plans. First, plans must not design covered benefits in ways that discriminate against individuals based on age, health status, or related factors. Second, plans must ensure an appropriate balance among the categories of EHB so that benefits are not unduly weighted toward any category. These rules apply to states as they select and supplement benchmark plans, as well as to insurers as they modify their own plan designs relative to the benchmark. The proposed rule does not elaborate at length on the definition of "discriminatory" or "balance," although it does specify that plan marketing practices and benefit designs should not have the effect of discouraging the enrollment of individuals with significant health needs. The proposed rule seeks comment on these issues and encourages states to develop programs and procedures to monitor for and correct discriminatory or unbalanced benefit designs.

2. Actuarial value - While all individual and small group health insurance policies must cover the EHB, plans can vary in the level of cost sharing they apply to covered benefits. The ACA requires plans to be designated according to categories, based on their actuarial value (AV), which is a measure of the overall level of cost sharing required under a plan. The AV categories specified in the ACA would reflect whether plans require low, medium, high, or very high levels of cost sharing. These categories, also referred to as metal tiers, are

- Bronze (for plans with an actuarial value of 60 percent)
- Silver (actuarial value of 70 percent)
- Gold (actuarial value of 80 percent)
- Platinum (actuarial value of 90 percent)

Insurers have flexibility to vary cost sharing features within these overall levels. For example, one insurer might design a bronze plan with an annual deductible of $4,350, followed by coinsurance of 80 percent, while a different insurer might design its bronze plan with an annual deductible of $2,750 followed by coinsurance of 70 percent. To standardize calculations of AV as much as possible, the proposed rule requires plans to use a common AV calculator developed by HHS. To the extent plans have cost sharing features that don't fit the parameters of the AV calculator, they are allowed make their own actuarial value calculations certified by an actuary.

The ACA also sets standards for the maximum cost-sharing (such as deductibles, co-pays, and coinsurance) that applies to EHBs provided in network. The annual out-of-pocket maximum for all types of cost sharing cannot exceed that established by the Internal Revenue Service for qualified high deductible health plans. That amount is indexed and updated each year; for 2014 it will be approximately $6,500 for a self-only policy, and $13,000 for a non-self-only policy. After the out-of-pocket maximum is reached, the plan must cover services at 100 percent for the remainder of the year. (Note that actuarial values and out-of-pocket limits apply only to in-network cost-sharing. There are no limits on out-of-network cost-sharing.)

In addition, for small group health plans, the ACA provides that deductibles cannot exceed $2,000 per year per individual. However, the rule notes that it may be difficult to design a bronze plan subject to this limit and the overall out-of-pocket limit, so it permits insurers to exceed the $2,000 small group policy deductible limit if they cannot reasonably reach an AV tier without doing so.

Overall, the EHB and AV standards will likely increase what health plans cover today and raise premiums for some policies as a result – especially in the individual market, where policies may impose very high cost sharing (such as annual deductibles of $10,000 or more) or lack coverage for key benefits such as maternity care, mental health care, rehabilitative services, and prescription drugs. The EHB and AV requirements are also intended to make health insurance more standardized. Standardization reinforces risk spreading by limiting opportunities to attract or discourage enrollees based on benefit design. It also simplifies the process of comparing health plans for consumers.

The proposed rule recognizes that standardization can also limit choice in benefit design and cause some market disruption to the extent new plan standards are very different from what is offered today. The proposed rule seeks to balance these tradeoffs, at least at the outset, by defining EHB in the context of existing benchmark plans that are familiar to many privately insured people today, and by allowing insurers flexibility to modify plan designs within constraints of the overall standards. It remains to be seen how insurers – who may be accustomed to using benefit design as a risk selection tool today – will use flexibility in reformed markets, and whether regulators will be able to monitor and correct such practices starting in 2014.

Wellness – Finally, the third proposed rule would amend an earlier, final regulation governing the design and application of wellness programs offered in connection with employer-sponsored group health plans. Wellness programs are intended to provide support and incentives to employees to adopt healthier lifestyles or take other actions to improve health and, by so doing, help to control health care costs. Since the enactment of HIPAA, which established the federal law that employer-sponsored group health plans cannot discriminate against group members based on health status, special exceptions have been permitted for wellness programs that offer discounts on premiums for health benefits, and these exceptions have evolved over time through regulatory and statutory interpretation.

Interim final rules to implement HIPAA, issued in 1997, permitted group health plans to establish premium discounts or rebates or to modify cost sharing under the plan in return for adherence to wellness programs. The 1997 rule made clear that under no circumstances could wellness programs condition receipt of the reward based on health-status-related factors. The 1997 rule noted, for example, that a program that provides premium discounts only to enrollees who can achieve a blood cholesterol count under 200 would be considered to discriminate impermissibly based on a health status-related factor.

In 2006, the Bush Administration reinterpreted the nondiscrimination rule and modified the wellness program exception for group health plans. The 2006 rule recognized two types of wellness programs – those that condition a reward based on an individual's ability to achieve a health-status-related factor, and those that do not. Health-factor based wellness programs would not be considered discriminatory if they met 5 standards:

- *Reasonably designed* – The rule defined a reasonably designed program as one that has a reasonable chance to promote health or prevent disease, is not overly burdensome, is not a subterfuge for discrimination based on health status, and is not highly suspect in the method chosen to promote health or prevent disease. The preamble to the 2006 rule stressed that the "reasonably designed" standard was designed to prevent abuse, but otherwise was "intended to be an easy standard to satisfy...There does not need to be a scientific record that the method promotes wellness to satisfy this standard. [It] is intended to allow experimentation in diverse ways of promoting wellness. For example a plan...could satisfy this standard by providing rewards to individual who participated in a course of aromatherapy."

- *Limit on the reward* – The 2006 rule said that under a health-factor based wellness program, the reward can be in the form of a discount or rebate of a premium or contribution, a waiver of all or part of a cost-sharing mechanisms (such as deductibles or copays), the absence of a surcharge, or the value of a benefit that would not otherwise be provided under the plan. The size of the reward could not exceed 20 percent of the entire cost (employer and employee contribution combined) of self-only coverage or, if spouses and children can participate in the program, of family coverage.

- *Reasonable alternative standard* – The 2006 rule required plans to also offer a reasonable alternative standard for obtaining the reward for certain individuals. The

31

alternative standard must be available for individuals for whom it is medically inadvisable or difficult to satisfy the otherwise applicable standard. The rule noted it is permissible for a plan to devise a reasonable alternative standard by lowering the threshold of the existing health-factor-related standard, substituting a different standard, or waiving the standard.

- *Opportunity to qualify for the reward* – Under the rule, individuals had to be given at least one opportunity each year to qualify for the reward.
- *Notice* – All plan materials that describe the terms of the program must also disclose the availability of a reasonable alternative standard.

In addition, the 2006 regulation specified that "Compliance with this section is not determinative of compliance with … any other State or Federal law, such as the Americans with Disabilities Act…" The ADA, for example, limits an employer's ability to even request information from employees about their health status related factors, including outside of a voluntary wellness program.

The Affordable Care Act codified the main features of the 2006 rules, changing one. It said wellness programs that establish incentives or rewards based on health-status-related factors are allowed, as long as they meet at least the five standards outlined in the 2006 regulation. The ACA increased the maximum allowable reward to 30 percent of the plan cost and gave the Secretary authority to increase it further to 50 percent. It also gave the Secretary authority to publish implementing regulations.

The wellness NPRM proposes amendments to the 2006 rule. It maintains a requirement of reasonable design, restating the 2006 language that this requirement is intended to be an easy standard to satisfy. Proposed amendments would change the 2006 standards in the following ways:

- *Limit on reward* – The proposed rule would increase to 30 percent the maximum reward allowable under reasonably designed programs. In addition, to the extent that a wellness program targets tobacco use and assigns at least 20 percentage points of the reward toward that goal, the maximum reward allowable could be 50 percent of plan costs.
- *Reasonable alternative standard* – The proposed rule makes several changes in this standard. First, it requires that all individuals who cannot satisfy the initial standard must be offered a reasonable alternative means to qualify for the reward. Employers have flexibility to design the reasonable alternative means; however, if the alternative involves a class or program that charges a membership fee, the employer must pay

that fee. In addition, an individual's physician has the final say on whether it is medically inadvisable for that person to satisfy the initial or alternative standard, and if so, a medically appropriate standard for that person must be offered or the standard must be waived.

The proposed rule offers illustrations of programs that would be considered reasonably designed. Under one example, the wellness program might offer a reward to any employee whose blood cholesterol level is under 200, but offer to anyone who fails that standard an alternative way to earn the reward by simply participating in a walking program three times a week, regardless of whether this results in actually lowering cholesterol levels. Whether other program designs would be considered reasonable is not so clearly spelled out or illustrated.

Allowing variation in health insurance premium contributions, cost sharing or benefits based on health status as an incentive to promote wellness, by definition, involves tradeoffs. On the one hand, if such programs effectively promote wellness and prevent disease, they could help limit overall health care spending and promote affordability of coverage. On the other hand, to the extent such programs make it more expensive for individuals with health problems to participate in group health plan benefits, they might also undermine risk pooling and promote loss of coverage for some individuals with poorer health status.

The KFF employer health benefits survey finds that while most employers offering health benefits today also offer wellness programs (for example, subsidizing gym memberships or providing smoking cessation classes), only 14 percent have adopted wellness incentives that involve health insurance premium or cost-sharing discounts for individuals who pass certain health standards. However, starting in 2014, other changes in the small group health insurance market could also change the context in which employers and insurers make decisions about wellness incentives. For example,

- Under the proposed rule, wellness programs would be allowed to condition rewards/penalties based on biometric measures, including blood glucose levels. As a result, under some plans, individuals with diabetes or pre-diabetes could have to pay thousands of dollars more per year to enroll in coverage. What practical opportunity insurers or plan sponsors may have to discourage enrollment of people with diabetes is not entirely clear. The NPRM notes that a reasonably designed program cannot be a subterfuge for discrimination based on health status, but it does not define "subterfuge" or specify standards or examples that would define or help identify impermissible program designs.

33

- Older workers potentially could face more costly wellness incentives. The market reform NPRM allows employers to assign to each worker their underlying cost of coverage, adjusted by age and tobacco use. That rule also permits flexibility for tobacco adjustments to vary by age (e.g., a 10 percent tobacco surcharge might apply for younger individuals but a 50 percent surcharge for older individuals.) The wellness NPRM doesn't specify whether or not employers and insurers could also vary wellness rewards and incentives by age.

- How wellness programs would interact with the employer responsibility provisions of the ACA has yet to be specified. The ACA requires that large employers must offer affordable health benefits; when an employee's contribution for coverage exceeds 9.5% of her income she can seek subsidized coverage in the Exchange and, if she does, her employer can be liable to pay a tax penalty. How will premium surcharges resulting from wellness programs be considered in determining the affordability of employer-sponsored coverage? Taking them into account might deter employers from adopting wellness programs with premium-based incentives as large as the ACA allows. Not taking them into account, though, could allow employers to set premium contributions that are less affordable for sicker employees without triggering tax penalties.

- Also yet to be spelled out is how wellness programs would interact with ACA standards for the actuarial value and minimum value of group health plans. The wellness NPRM allows deductibles and other cost sharing to vary by up to 50 percent of total plan cost, which could amount to thousands of dollars for an individual. Under the ACA, however, the annual per person deductible under small group health plans may not exceed $2000. The ACA also limits total cost sharing for an individual in a year to roughly $6500 in 2014. Could wellness programs result in some group plan participants facing cost sharing above these limits? The ACA also sets actuarial value standards for plans which, essentially, measure plan cost sharing. Large employer plans are required to offer a minimum value (MV) of 60 percent. Would the AV or MV standard for a plan be evaluated taking into account wellness incentives, or without regard to them?

Finally, it is not clear how employer-sponsored wellness programs authorized under ERISA may be treated under other federal laws, such as the Americans with Disabilities Act (ADA.) The ADA, for example, prohibits employers from collecting health information about employees except under limited circumstances. One exception is when information is collected as part of a voluntary wellness program. Would wellness programs authorized under the ACA be considered voluntary under the ADA? The NPRM notes that the wellness program reward can take the form of the absence of a surcharge. In such programs, all employees could be considered to be auto enrolled in the penalty, and only those who enroll in the wellness program and meet its standards can qualify for the reward. Regulations defining "voluntary" under the ADA have yet to be issued, so the answer to this question remains open for now.

Conclusion

Overall, the market reform rules would likely lead to significant changes in private health insurance compared to how it is sold today. Requirements for guaranteed issue, guaranteed renewability, and modified community rating would prevent insurers from turning people down or charging them more based on health status, making insurance more accessible and affordable for people who have expensive health conditions. The proposed regulation's requirement that insurers consolidate all of their products in a market into a single risk pool reinforces risk spreading, as does the requirement that association coverage follow the rules that apply in traditional individual and small group markets.

While risk spreading equalizes access to coverage for all market participants, relative to how most state insurance markets operate today, these market reforms inevitably have redistributive impacts. The most dramatic effects will surely occur in the individual market, where older and sicker individuals face many barriers to coverage today. Taking down those barriers and requiring individual health insurance to provide more comprehensive coverage will likely raise premiums relative to those charged today, particularly for participants who are younger and healthier. However, in 2014 premium subsidies will also be offered through new Exchanges, and most individuals who buy in these new markets will qualify for subsidies, shielding them from these redistributions.

In 2014, it will continue to be the case that most privately insured people will be covered by employer-sponsored group health plans. In such plans, risk pooling tends to occur more naturally, some key market reforms, such as nondiscrimination, have long been in place, and employer premium contributions help stabilize risk pools by making coverage affordable for most participants. Under the new proposed rules, however, some key exceptions to risk pooling within groups are allowed in order to promote other goals – increasing take up rates of younger workers and promoting personal health responsibility and wellness. How these exceptions are ultimately implemented could have significant implications for the affordability of coverage for people who are older or in poorer health.

CHAPTER THREE

The Law and You

Since the signing of the bill into law, we've been hearing about Obamacare but many people are still very confused about what it's about, and what it really means for them. Here's a breakdown of how the Affordable Care Act affects you:

The uninsured

Starting in 2014, you will be required to purchase insurance or pay a penalty of as much as 2.5% of your income. If you make more than four times the federal poverty level ($88,000 for a family of four) you will now have to buy coverage and pay the whole premium. If your income is lower, the good news is that Medicaid, the government plan for the poor, will expand to cover you plus 14 million other people, but only those making less than 133% of the federal poverty level will be completely covered. You can shop for the insurance that meets your needs on a state-run exchange.

Exchanges will allow you to compare health plans before you buy one. The exchanges will also help you find out if you qualify for tax credits or other government health benefits. States are being given substantial Federal grants to fund the exchanges.

The insured

For the other 256 million Americans who already have health insurance through their employers or another source, the impact isn't as dramatic. Parents will still get to keep kids on their insurance plans up to age 26 and many insurers will continue to offer preventative services, such as immunizations, without co-pay. If anything, your premiums should decrease over time, as Obamacare is designed to lower health care costs. By allowing parents to add their children, more healthy people are paying premiums but not using the system as much.

This adds to health insurance companies' profits, which should mean lower premiums over the long run. Similarly, Medicare recipients now have more of their prescription costs covered, allowing them to continue taking medications needed to prevent emergency room visits.

By 2014, everyone will be required to have health insurance. This means that more people will use preventative medical care, instead of waiting until they have to go to the emergency room. The average emergency room visit is $1,265, and hospitals have to eat this cost for indigent patients. When these costs are transferred to insurance companies or prevented, hospital costs, and therefore overall health care costs, will drop.

Seniors

The new law protects guaranteed Medicare benefits. It also improves and expands those benefits, such as lower out-of-pocket drug costs and free Medicare-covered preventative care benefits. Yet another benefit is improved access to primary care doctors. In addition, Seniors who fell in the "doughnut hole"—the gap in Medicare's prescription drug coverage—will continue to get discounts on their medications.

Meanwhile Medicare Advantage plans—private insurers, which currently attract almost one in four seniors, will see enrollment cut roughly in half over the next 10 years. That could be bad news for the Senior citizens who've signed up with **Humana** (HUM - news - people), the AARP plan run by **UnitedHealth Group** (UNH - news - people), or another carrier, in order to avoid paying the $96 a month for Medicare's Part B program or to avoid the $1,100 hospitalization deductible. Since there are serious gaps in Medicare coverage, including the absence of catastrophic protection, roughly nine out of 10 seniors on traditional Medicare already need to purchase supplemental insurance, such as Medigap.

Top Things to Know for Seniors

- Under the health care law, your existing guaranteed Medicare-covered benefits won't be reduced or taken away. Neither will your ability to choose your own doctor.
- Nearly 4 million people with Medicare received cost relief during the law's first year. If you had Medicare prescription drug coverage and had to pay for your drugs in the coverage gap known as the "donut hole," you received a one-time, tax free $250 rebate from Medicare to help pay for your prescriptions.

- If you have high prescription drug costs that put you in the donut hole, you now get a 50% discount on covered brand-name drugs while you're in the donut hole. Between today and 2020, you'll get continuous Medicare coverage for your prescription drugs. The donut hole will be closed completely by 2020.
- Medicare covers certain preventive services without charging you the Part B coinsurance or deductible. You will also be offered a free annual wellness exam.
- The life of the Medicare Trust Fund will be extended as a result of reducing waste, fraud and abuse, and slowing cost growth in Medicare, which will provide you with future cost savings on your premiums and coinsurance.
- ObamaCare reigns excess spending on Medicare Advantage, which is currently causing a burden on the tax payer that is disproportionate to the amount of people it helps. Medicare Advantage is run by private insurers and cots $1,000 more per person than traditional Medicare. ObamaCare reduces payments to Medicare advantage rewarding those providers who increase the quality of their coverage.

Young adults

Young adults have historically had the highest uninsured rate of any age group. One of the first coverage provisions in the Affordable Care Act to take effect was the extension of dependent coverage, which enables young adults up to age 26 to be covered through a parent's private health insurance plan. This coverage is available to young adults who do not have employment-based coverage even if they are not students, live away from their parents, and are not financially dependent on their parents. This policy is already increasing the number of young adults with health insurance. "Longer term, better access to healthcare while young is likely to translate to better health later in life, especially for people with serious medical conditions", , says Benjamin D. Sommers an assistant professor of health policy and economics at the Harvard School of Public Health and Brigham & Women's Hospital, in Boston. "An added benefit is that being able to stay on their parents' plan means that many young adults can pursue schooling or new job opportunities instead of having to make job decisions solely based on where they can get health insurance," he adds.

Top Things to Know for Young Adults

- Under the Affordable Care Act, you can now be insured as a dependent on your parent's health insurance if you're under age 26. The only exception is if your parent has an existing job-based plan and you can get your own job-based coverage.
- New health plans must now cover certain preventive services without cost sharing.

- Starting in 2014, if you're unemployed with limited income up to about $15,000 per year for a single person (higher income for couples/families with children), you may be eligible for health coverage through Medicaid.
- Starting in 2014, if your employer doesn't offer insurance, you will be able to buy insurance directly in an Affordable Insurance Exchange. An Exchange is a new transparent and competitive insurance marketplace where individuals and small businesses can buy affordable and qualified health benefit plans. Exchanges will offer you a choice of health plans that meet certain benefits and cost standards. Starting in 2014, members of Congress will be getting their health care insurance through Exchanges, and you will be able buy your insurance through Exchanges, too.
- Starting in 2014, if your income is less than the equivalent of about $43,000 for a single individual and your job doesn't offer affordable coverage, you may get tax credits to help pay for insurance.

Families

You do your best to keep your children healthy, but sickness and accidents are a part of life. Getting health insurance for your children gives you peace of mind knowing they have health coverage when they need it. But for many hardworking families, affordable insurance can be hard to find. The Affordable Care Act is giving you more control over your family's health care by expanding your options for health insurance and making them more affordable.

Top Things to Know for Families with Children

- Insurance companies can no longer impose lifetime dollar limits on essential coverage limits
- Job-based health plans and new individual plans are no longer allowed to deny or exclude coverage for your children (under age 19) based on a pre-existing condition, including a disability. Starting in 2014, these same plans won't be allowed to deny or exclude anyone or charge more for a pre-existing condition including a disability.
- Parents have new options to cover their children. If your children are under age 26, you can generally insure them if your policy allows for dependent coverage. The only exception is if you have an existing job-based plan, and your children can get their own job-based coverage.
- An Affordable Insurance Exchange is a new marketplace where individuals and small businesses can buy affordable health benefit plans. Exchanges will offer you a choice of plans that meet certain benefits and cost standards. Starting in 2014, members of Congress will be getting their health care insurance through Exchanges, and you will be able buy your insurance through Exchanges, too.
- Pregnancy and newborn care, along with vision and dental coverage for children, will be covered in all Exchange plans and new plans sold to individuals and small businesses, starting in 2014.
- In 2014, if your income is less than the equivalent of about $88,000 for a family of four today, and your job doesn't offer affordable coverage, you may get tax credits to help pay for insurance.

People with pre-existing conditions

Since the law remains in place, the requirement that insurers cover people with pre-existing medical conditions remains active. The law also established that children under the age of 19 could no longer have limited benefits or be denied benefits because they had a pre-existing condition.

Starting in 2014, the law makes it illegal for any health insurance plan to use pre-existing conditions to exclude, limit or set unrealistic rates on coverage. It also established national high-risk pools that people with such conditions could join sooner to get health insurance.

More than 13 million American non-elderly adults have been denied insurance specifically because of their medical conditions, according to the Commonwealth Fund. The Kaiser Family Foundation says 21% of people who apply for health insurance on their own get turned down, are charged a higher price, or offered a plan that excludes coverage for their pre-existing condition.

Middle income Americans

The Average American (those making under 400% FLP) will most likely see a reduction in their insurance premiums and 30 of the 44 million without insurance will gain access coverage via the "ObamaCare" exchanges, Medicare or Medicaid.

ObamaCare offers a number of protections and benefits that range from chipping away at preexisting conditions to expanding health services. Overall the quality of health care is increased, while the cost, in theory, will be reduced. Middle income Americans (those making between 133% - 400% of the federal poverty level), and employees will be able to use tax credits and subsidies on the exchanges to save up to 60% of the current cost of premiums making insurance affordable to up to 23 million Americans.

One of the cons of ObamaCare is that since many Americans work for larger employers, some employees may have the new costs involved with insuring their workforce passed onto them. Other workers will see a decrease in quality of plans offered by employers, to avoid the employer paying a excise tax on high-end health insurance plans. These cons will affect less than 1% of businesses, and only a small fraction will deal with the new challenges by cutting worker hours, benefits or not hiring new workers.

Healthy Individuals

The health care law helps improve care and lower costs for healthy individuals and people with health conditions. Even if you're healthy now, sooner or later there will come a time when you will need health insurance. Not having health insurance when you need it can result in large amounts of debt and bad credit ratings. Worrying about health insurance and the cost of your care is the last thing you want to do. The Affordable Care Act is expanding your options for health insurance and making them more affordable.

Top Things to Know for Healthy Individuals

- Under the health care law, insurance companies can no longer drop you when you get sick just because you made a mistake on your coverage application.
- Parents have new options to cover their children. If you have children under age 26, you can insure them if your policy allows for dependent coverage. The only exception is if you have an existing job-based plan, and your children can get their own job-based coverage.
- Job-based health plans and new individual plans are no longer allowed to deny or exclude coverage to any child under age 19 based on health conditions, including babies born with health problems.
- Starting in 2014, if your income is less than the equivalent of about $88,000 for a family of four today and your job doesn't offer affordable coverage, you may get tax credits to help pay for insurance.
- Starting in 2014, if your employer doesn't offer insurance, you will be able to buy insurance directly in an Exchange that gives you power similar to what large businesses and members of Congress have to get better choices and lower prices.

People with Disabilities

If you're living with a disability, private health insurance may be hard to come by. Even if you can afford to buy it, it probably doesn't cover all of your needs. Worrying about where to get coverage and the cost of your care is the last thing you want to do. The Affordable Care Act is expanding your options for health insurance and making them more affordable.

Top Things to Know for People with Disabilities

- Under the health care law, job-based and new individual plans are no longer allowed to deny or exclude coverage to any child under age 19 based on a pre-existing condition, including a disability.
- Starting in 2014, these same plans won't be able to exclude anyone from coverage or charge a higher premium for a pre-existing condition including a disability.
- Insurance companies can no longer drop you when you get sick just because you made a mistake on your coverage application.
- Insurance companies can no longer impose lifetime dollar limits on your coverage.
- Medicaid covers many people with disabilities now, and in the future it will provide insurance to even more Americans.
- Starting in 2014, most adults under age 65 with incomes up to about $15,000 per year for single individual (higher income for couples/families with children) will qualify for Medicaid in every state. State Medicaid programs will also be able to offer additional services to help those who need long-term care at home and in the community.
- You may be able to join and get benefits from a voluntary, enrollment-based insurance program that will be available after October 2012 called the Community Living Assistance Services and Supports (CLASS) Program.

Individuals with Health Conditions

If you have a health condition, you know how important having health insurance is and how expensive it can be. Worrying about where to get coverage and the cost of your care is the last thing you want to do when you are dealing with chronic illness. The health care law is expanding your options for health insurance and making them more affordable.

Top Things to Know for Individuals with Health Conditions

- Under the health care law, if you have been uninsured for at least six months and have a health condition, you may be able to get health insurance through the Pre-Existing Condition Insurance Plan.
- If a new insurance plan doesn't pay for services you believe were covered, you now have new, clear options to appeal the decision.
- Insurance companies can no longer drop you if you get sick just because you made a mistake on your coverage application.
- Starting in 2014, job-based and new individual plans won't be able to exclude you from coverage or charge you a higher premium for a pre-existing condition, including a disability.
- Starting in 2014, if your income is less than the equivalent of about $88,000 for a family of four today, and your job doesn't offer affordable coverage, you may get tax credits to help pay for insurance

Pregnant Women

Pregnancy is an exciting time. You're busy taking care of yourself and preparing for the arrival of your child. Worrying about health insurance and the cost of care is the last thing you want to do. The Affordable Care Act expands your options for health insurance and makes them more affordable.

Top Things to Know for Pregnant Women

- Job-based health plans and new individual plans are no longer allowed to deny or exclude coverage to your baby (or any child under age 19) based on health conditions, including babies born with health problems.
- New health plans must now cover certain preventive services without cost sharing.
- Starting in 2014, essential health benefits such as pregnancy and newborn care, along with vision and dental care for children, will be covered in all new individual, small business and Exchange plans.
- Starting in 2014, job-based health plans and new individual plans won't be allowed to deny or exclude anyone or charge more for a pre-existing condition, including pregnancy or a disability.
- In 2014, if your income is less than the equivalent of about $88,000 for a family of four today and your job doesn't offer affordable coverage, you may get tax credits to help pay for insurance.

Small Businesses

Obamacare requires businesses with 50 or more employees to provide health insurance. If you have fewer than 100 employees, you can shop for insurance in state-run exchanges in 2014 that should provide cheaper alternatives than are available now. If you refuse to provide insurance, you will be fined $2,000 per employee for all but the first 20 employees. However, businesses with 25 employees or less who provide insurance can qualify for a tax credit (35% now, 50% in 2014). If you have fewer than 50 employees, you don't have to pay a fine if your workers get tax credits through an exchange. If you offer health insurance as a benefit to early retirees 55-64, you can get Federal financial assistance.

Top Things to Know for Small Businesses

- If you have up to 25 employees, pay average annual wages below $50,000, and provide health insurance, you may qualify for a small business tax credit of up to 35% (up to 25% for non-profits) to offset the cost of your insurance. This will bring down the cost of providing insurance.
- Under the health care law, employer-based plans that provide health insurance to retirees ages 55-64 can now get financial help through the Early Retiree Reinsurance Program. This program is designed to lower the cost of premiums for all employees and reduce employer health costs.
- Starting in 2014, the small business tax credit goes up to 50% (up to 35% for non-profits) for qualifying businesses. This will make the cost of providing insurance even lower.
- In 2014, small businesses with generally fewer than 100 employees can shop in an Affordable Insurance Exchange, which gives you power similar to what large businesses have to get better choices and lower prices. An Exchange is a new marketplace where individuals and small businesses can buy affordable health benefit plans.
- Exchanges will offer a choice of plans that meet certain benefits and cost standards. Starting in 2014, members of Congress will be getting their health care insurance through Exchanges, and you will be able to buy your insurance through Exchanges, too.
- Employers with fewer than 50 employees are exempt from new employer responsibility policies. They don't have to pay an assessment if their employees get tax credits through an Exchange.

Self-Employed

There's good and bad news. The bad: Yes, the PPACA will require most people to buy health insurance starting in 2014. It will also create more and more affordable, options for doing so. Some states consider self-employed people small businesses, and allow them to buy the health insurance for small a employer that's available. Your State Department of Insurance can tell you if you qualify. If your state doesn't consider self-employed people small businesses, Healthcare.gov's insurance and coverage finder can help you find an individual plan.

Starting in 2014, you may be eligible for government subsidies to make insurance more affordable. Self-employed people earning less than four times the poverty level will qualify. (In 2010, four times the poverty level was about $43,000 for an individual and $88,000 for a family of four.)

Religious liberty

With the exception of churches and houses of worship, the Patient Protection and Affordable Care Act mandates contraceptive coverage for all employers and educational institutions, even though the mandate itself is not included in the wording of the law(s) passed by Congress. The mandate applies to all new health insurance plans effective August 2012. It controversially includes Christian hospitals, Christian charities, Catholic universities, and other enterprises owned or controlled by religious organizations that oppose contraception on doctrinal grounds. Regulations made under the act rely on the recommendations of the Institute of Medicine, which concluded that birth control is medically necessary "to ensure women's health and well-being." The United States Conference of Catholic Bishops has since taken the lead in opposition to the regulations Cardinal Timothy M. Dolan, the archbishop of New York and president of the United States Conference of Catholic Bishops stated that the provision "represents a challenge and a compromise of our religious liberty". Other organizations, such as Planned Parenthood, supported the provision. The Evangelical Lutheran Church in America, The Presbyterian Church (USA), Reform Judaism, the United Methodist Church, and the United Church of Christ all have said they support the Mandate and all offer these products on their health plans. The regulations issued under the act are also opposed by active Christian Evangelicals.

The Obama administration proposed changes in response to the criticism. Under the proposed new regulation, birth control medication would be provided by the insurers, without direct involvement by the religious organization. On March 16, 2012, regulations were issued which ensure coverage for employees of enterprises controlled by religious institutions that self-insure. Regulations were also issued which require coverage for students at institutions controlled by religious organizations which purchase insurance. It is believed by the federal government that it is not possible under current law to require contraceptive coverage for students at institutions controlled by religious organizations which self-insure

CHAPTER FOUR

Supreme Confusion: The Individual Mandate in Context

Three years ago, virtually no one knowledgeable in US constitutional law seriously doubted the constitutionality of the individual mandate, the key financial provision of the Affordable Care Act-- a device first conceived by Republicans and the conservative Heritage Foundation in the 1980s as a means of lowering the cost of health care while maintaining insurance as free enterprise and avoiding the "socialised medicine" that is preferred in Europe. But all that changed as soon as Barack Obama and the Democrats embraced it - confounding their assumption that the way to gain broad bipartisan support was to adopt some Republican ideas.

Following the signing of the Patient Protection and Affordable Care Act into law in March 2010, a number of parties sued, claiming that the sweeping reform law was unconstitutional for various reasons. At the Supreme Court, these separate cases were merged into a single case titled *National Federation of Independent Business v. Sebelius.*

National Federation of Independent Business v. Sebelius, 567 U.S. ___ (2012), was a landmark United States Supreme Court decision in which the Court upheld Congress's power to enact most provisions of the Patient Protection and Affordable Care Act (ACA) and the Health Care and Education Reconciliation Act (HCERA), including a requirement for most Americans to have health insurance by 2014. The Acts represented a major set of changes to the American health care system that had been the subject of highly contentious debate, largely divided on political party lines.

The Commerce Clause

Central to the court's decision was its interpretation of the mandate *vis-à-vis* "the Commerce Clause", which is the clause in the US constitution that empowers Congress to regulate interstate trade. Congress only has the power to regulate between states. Otherwise, that power, according to the constitution, is left to the states. Central to that question was whether

47

Congress was regulating a market that already existed, which was the government's view, or one that did not already exist, which was the plaintiff's view.

The Commerce Clause argument was valid if the market did exist, invalid if it did not. Most legal experts, including Ronald Reagan's solicitor general Charles Fried, assumed a market already existed - because, after all, everyone needs health care - and that the individual mandate, therefore, was on sound constitutional footing. However, an epic propaganda campaign led by the US Chamber of Commerce, libertarian activists bankrolled by billionaires and health insurance companies - who stand to gain customers but lose millions in the long term - shifted the frame of the debate so that we were no longer talking about "health care", but instead we were talking about "health insurance".

This is not just semantics. It made all the difference to five Justices, including Roberts, who viewed Congress as creating a market, which it has no power to do. Roberts said [PDF]:

> "Congress already possesses expansive power to regulate what people do. Upholding the Affordable Care Act under the Commerce Clause would give Congress the same license to regulate what people do not do. The Framers ... gave Congress the power to *regulate* commerce, not to *compel* it. Ignoring that distinction would undermine the principle that the federal government is a government of limited and enumerated powers. The individual mandate thus cannot be sustained under Congress's power to 'regulate Commerce'."

Regarding the argument that the mandate penalizes or taxes "inactivity", Roberts wrote:

> ...it is abundantly clear the Constitution does not guarantee that individuals may avoid taxation through inactivity. A capitation, after all, is a tax that everyone must pay simply for existing, and capitations are expressly contemplated by the Constitution. The Court today holds that our Constitution protects us from federal regulation under the Commerce Clause so long as we abstain from the regulated activity. But from its creation, the Constitution has made no such promise with respect to taxes.

Further, five Justices including Roberts would have held that the individual mandate was unsupported by the Necessary and Proper Clause (Art. I, §8, cl. 18).

The Court narrowed the Medicaid penalty provision by ruling that the federal government could not withhold existing Medicaid funding from states that choose not to participate the

Act's extension of the Medicaid program. Justices Roberts, Breyer, and Kagan concluded that punishing states for failure to comply in the Medicaid expansion by withholding existing Medicaid funding (42 U.S.C. §1396c) is unconstitutional. Roberts noted "[the] constitutional violation is fully remedied by precluding [Sebelius] from applying §1396c to withdraw existing Medicaid funds for failure to comply with the requirements set out the expansion", leaving the other provisions of the ACA unaffected.

Chief Justice Roberts concluded:

> The Affordable Care Act is constitutional in part and unconstitutional in part. The individual mandate cannot be upheld as an exercise of Congress's power under the Commerce Clause. That Clause authorizes Congress to regulate interstate commerce, not to order individuals to engage in it. In this case, however, it is reasonable to construe what Congress has done as increasing taxes on those who have a certain amount of income, but choose to go without health insurance. Such legislation is within Congress's power to tax.

> As for the Medicaid expansion, that portion of the Affordable Care Act violates the Constitution by threatening existing Medicaid funding. Congress has no authority to order the States to regulate according to its instructions. Congress may offer the States grants and require the States to comply with accompanying conditions, but the States must have a genuine choice whether to accept the offer.

> ...

> The Federal Government does not have the power to *order people* to buy health insurance. Section 5000A [of the Internal Revenue Code] would therefore be unconstitutional *if* read as a command. The Federal Government *does* have the power to *impose a tax* on those without health insurance. Section 5000A is therefore constitutional, because it can reasonably be read *as a tax*

And this is where it gets interesting, and this is why both *CNN* and *Fox News* misreported the court's ruling the day after , sending some viewers, reportedly including the president, into apoplexy: Roberts said he believed the law was not constitutional under the Commerce Clause, but that it was constitutional under taxing power afforded to Congress under the constitution. If you don't buy health insurance, then, under the mandate, you pay a penalty. But that penalty was never defined. Roberts reasoned that this was like a tax - buy health insurance and don't pay a tax; don't buy health insurance and pay a tax. Either way, you can't avoid a benefit or penalty, or this, he said, was in keeping with the constitution.

This is why *CNN* and *Fox News* initially reported that the law had been struck down, because Roberts said that the Commerce Clause argument was invalid. But in the rush to be the first to report the decision, they didn't see that later in his opinion - on the fourth page - Roberts said the mandate was constitutional, because it's more like a tax than anything else.

Regulating regulation

And this is where it gets even more interesting, legally speaking. Saying Congress does not have the power to regulate a market that is blindingly already there to anyone paying attention - because, after all, everyone needs health care - Roberts has opened the door to scuttling the federal government's power to regulate anything. As Tom Scocca in *Slate* put it:

> "This is a substantial rollback of Congress' regulatory powers, and the chief justice knows it ... In 2005, Senator Barack Obama spoke in opposition to Roberts' nomination, saying he did not trust his political philosophy on tough questions such as "whether the Commerce Clause empowers Congress to speak on those issues of broad national concern that may be only tangentially related to what is easily defined as interstate commerce". Today, Roberts did what Obama predicted he would do."

Politically, Republicans are now in the spin zone: They now say that Obama and the Democrats tried to tax US voters without telling them it was a tax, and that it took the highest court in the land to reveal it. There is some merit to the claim. Chief Justice Roberts did say the mandate was like a tax, but there are two ways of looking at this.

One is that this is a distinction without a difference. Either you pay for insurance or you pay a penalty (tax). That's not the same as the government raising revenues from sales or income taxes. You get something in return that you actually need; you just needed a little encouragement to do it. As Charles Fried, Reagan's top lawyer, told the *Washington Post* in March, there is no difference between making you buy something (or pay a penalty) and taxing you and then giving the money back. The only difference is that free-market US capitalists prefer the former, while European democratic socialists preferred the latter.

Payroll taxes work in the same way. That money, proportional to your income, is set aside for when you are old and sick. You get something for that money, but it isn't just Social Security and Medicare. You get an entitlement. This is how Franklin Roosevelt explained Social Security: "We put those payroll contributions there, so as to give the contributors a legal, moral and political right to collect their pensions ... With those taxes in there, no damn politician can ever scrap my social security program."

Conservative wants us to believe taxation is always bad, but it isn't, and for this reason, we may eventually see that, there is no going back. Not after Americans come to see that they are paying for the legal, moral and political right to good health.

How the "mandate" will affect you

Under the Affordable Care Act, the federal government, state governments, insurers, employers, and individuals are given shared responsibility to reform and improve the availability, quality, and affordability of health insurance coverage in the United States. Starting in 2014, the individual shared responsibility provision calls for each individual to have minimum essential health coverage (known as minimum essential coverage) for each month, qualify for an exemption, or make a payment when filing his or her federal income tax return.

The provision applies to individuals of all ages, including children. The adult or married couple who can claim a child or another individual as a dependent for federal income tax purposes is responsible for making the payment if the dependent does not have coverage or an exemption.

1. What counts as minimum essential coverage?

Minimum essential coverage includes at a minimum all of the following:

- Employer-sponsored coverage (including COBRA coverage and retiree coverage)
- Coverage purchased in the individual market
- Medicare coverage (including Medicare Advantage)
- Medicaid coverage
- Children's Health Insurance Program (CHIP) coverage
- Certain types of Veterans health coverage

- TRICARE

Minimum essential coverage does not include specialized coverage, such as coverage only for vision care or dental care, workers' compensation, disability policies, or coverage only for a specific disease or condition.

The Department of Health and Human Services (HHS) has authority to designate additional types of coverage as minimum essential coverage..

2. What are the statutory exemptions from the requirement to obtain minimum essential coverage?

1. **Religious conscience:** You are a member of a religious sect that is recognized as conscientiously opposed to accepting any insurance benefits. The Social Security Administration administers the process for recognizing these sects according to the criteria in the law.

2. **Health care sharing ministry:** You are a member of a recognized health care sharing ministry.

3. **Indian tribes:** You are a member of a federally recognized Indian tribe.

4. **No filing requirement:** Your household income is below the minimum threshold for filing a tax return. The requirement to file a federal tax return depends on your filing status, age, and types and amounts of income. To find out if you are required to file a federal tax return, use the IRS Interactive Tax Assistant (ITA).

5. **Short coverage gap:** You went without coverage for less than three consecutive months during the year. For more information see question 21.

6. **Hardship:** A Health Insurance Marketplace, also known as an Affordable Insurance Exchange, has certified that you have suffered a hardship that makes you unable to obtain coverage.

7. **Unaffordable coverage options:** You can't afford coverage because the minimum amount you must pay for the premiums is more than eight percent of your household income.

8. **Incarceration:** You are in a jail, prison, or similar penal institution or correctional facility after the disposition of charges against you.

9. **Not lawfully present:** You are neither a U.S. citizen, a U.S. national, nor an alien lawfully present in the U.S.

3. What do I need to do if I want to be sure I have minimum essential coverage or an exemption for 2014?

Most individuals in the United States have health coverage today that will count as minimum essential coverage and will not need to do anything more than continue the coverage that they have. For those who do not have coverage, who anticipate discontinuing the coverage they have currently, or who want to explore whether more affordable options are available, Health Insurance Marketplaces (also know as Affordable Insurance Exchanges) will open for every state and the District of Columbia in October of 2013. These Health Insurance Marketplaces will help qualified individuals find minimum essential coverage that fits their budget and potentially financial assistance to help with the costs of coverage beginning in 2014. The Health Insurance Marketplace will also be able to assess whether applicants are eligible for Medicaid or the Children's Health Insurance Program (CHIP). For those who will become eligible for Medicare during 2013, enrolling for Medicare will also ensure that you have minimum essential coverage for 2014.

For those seeking an exemption, a Health Insurance Marketplace will be able to provide certificates of exemption for many of the exemption categories. HHS has proposed regulations on how a Health Insurance Marketplace will go about granting these exemptions. Individuals will also be able to claim exemptions for 2014 when they file their federal income tax returns in 2015. Individuals who are not required to file a federal income tax return are automatically exempt and do not need to take any further action to secure an exemption. See question 20 for further information on exemptions.

Who is Affected?

4. Are children subject to the individual shared responsibility provision?

Yes. Each child must have minimum essential coverage or qualify for an exemption for each month in the calendar year. Otherwise, the adult or married couple who can claim the child as a dependent for federal income tax purposes will owe a payment.

5. Are senior citizens subject to the individual shared responsibility provision?

Yes. Senior citizens must have minimum essential coverage or qualify for an exemption for each month in a calendar year. Senior citizens will have minimum essential coverage for every month they are enrolled in Medicare.

6. Are all individuals living in the United States subject to the individual shared responsibility provision?

All citizens are subject to the individual shared responsibility provision as are all permanent residents and all foreign nationals who are in the United States long enough during a calendar year to qualify as resident aliens for tax purposes. Foreign nationals who live in the United States for a short enough period that they do not become resident aliens for federal income tax purposes are not subject to the individual shared responsibility payment even though they may have to file a US income tax return.

7. Are US citizens living abroad subject to the individual shared responsibility provision?

Yes. However, US citizens who live abroad for a calendar year (or at least 330 days within a 12 month period) are treated as having minimum essential coverage for the year (or period). These are individuals who qualify for an exclusion from income under section 911 of the Code.

8. Are residents of the territories subject to the individual shared responsibility provision?

All bona fide residents of the United States territories are treated by law as having minimum essential coverage. They are not required to take any action to comply with the individual shared responsibility provision.

Minimum Essential Coverage

9. If I receive my coverage from my spouse's employer, will I have minimum essential coverage?

Yes. Employer-sponsored coverage is generally minimum essential coverage. (See question 4 for information on specialized types of coverage that are not minimum essential coverage.) If an employee enrolls in employer-sponsored coverage for himself and his family, the employee and all of the covered family members have minimum essential coverage.

10. Do my spouse and dependent children have to be covered under the same policy or plan that covers me?

No. You, your spouse and your dependent children do not have to be covered under the same policy or plan. However, you, your spouse and each dependent child for whom you may claim a personal exemption on your federal income tax return must have minimum essential coverage or qualify for an exemption, or you will owe a payment when you file.

11. My employer tells me that our company's health plan is "grandfathered." Does my employer's plan provide minimum essential coverage?

Yes. Grandfathered group health plans provide minimum essential coverage.

12. I am a retiree, and I am too young to be eligible for Medicare. I receive my health coverage through a retiree plan made available by my former employer. Is the retiree plan minimum essential coverage?

Yes. Retiree health plans are generally minimum essential coverage.

13. I work for a local government that provides me with health coverage. Is my coverage minimum essential coverage?

Yes. Employer-sponsored coverage is minimum essential coverage regardless of whether the employer is a governmental, nonprofit, or for-profit entity.

14. Do I have to be covered for an entire calendar month in order to get credit for having minimum essential coverage for that month?

No. You will be treated as having minimum essential coverage for a month as long as you have coverage for at least one day during that month.

15. If I change health coverage during the year and end up with a gap when I am not covered, will I owe a payment?

Individuals are treated as having minimum essential coverage for a calendar month if they have coverage for at least one day during that month. Additionally, as long as the gap in coverage is less than three months, you may qualify for an exemption and not owe a payment. See question 21 for more information on the exemption for short coverage gaps.

Exemptions

16. If I think I qualify for an exemption, how do I claim it?

It depends upon which exemption it is.

- The religious conscience exemption and the hardship exemption are available only by going to a Health Insurance Marketplace, also known as an Affordable Insurance Exchange, and applying for an exemption certificate.
- The exemptions for members of Indian tribes, members of health care sharing ministries, and individuals who are incarcerated are available either by going to a Marketplace or Exchange and applying for an exemption certificate or by claiming the exemption as part of filing a federal income tax return.
- The exemptions for unaffordable coverage, short coverage gaps, and individuals who are not lawfully present in the United States can be claimed only as part of filing a federal income tax return. The exemption for those under the federal income tax return filing threshold is available automatically. No special action is needed.

17. What qualifies as a short coverage gap?

In general, a gap in coverage that lasts less than three months qualifies as a short coverage gap. If an individual has two short coverage gaps during a year, the short coverage gap exemption only applies to the first or earlier gap.

18. If my income is so low that I am not required to file a federal income tax return, do I need to do anything special to claim an exemption from the individual shared responsibility provision?

No. Individuals who are not required to file a tax return for a year are automatically exempt from owing a shared responsibility payment for that year and do not need to take any further action to secure an exemption.

Reporting Coverage or Exemptions or Making Payments

19. Will I have to do something on my federal income tax return to show that I had coverage or an exemption?

The individual shared responsibility provision goes into effect in 2014. You will not have to account for coverage or exemptions or to make any payments until you file your 2014 federal income tax return in 2015. Information will be made available later about how the income tax return will take account of coverage and exemptions. Insurers will be required to provide everyone that they cover each year with information that will help them demonstrate they had coverage.

20. What happens if I do not have minimum essential coverage, and I cannot afford to make the payment with my tax return?

The IRS routinely works with taxpayers who owe amounts they cannot afford to pay. The law prohibits the IRS from using liens or levies to collect any payment you owe related to the individual responsibility provision, if you, your spouse or a dependent included on your tax return does not have minimum essential coverage.

CHAPTER FIVE

Appling For Health Insurance

How does ObamaCare work? With the Insurance Exchange Pools opening in 2013 the question on our minds is, "How does ObamaCare work for me, my family and my business." The first thing you need to know about ObamaCare (The Affordable Health Care Act) is that you will either need to decide to keep your current insurance plan or purchase an insurance plan through an online marketplace otherwise known as an health insurance exchange pool.

Health insurance will be made available through the ObamaCare Health Insurance Exchange Pool. The exchange is a group of health insurance providers that will offer coverage. You will choose the provider you want for you, your family or business based off of who offers the most attractive package in regards of affordability and quality of coverage.

By 2014, each state must have an American Health Benefit Exchange and a Small Business Health Options Program Exchange in place. At these exchanges, individuals and businesses with fewer than 101 employees can choose from four different tiers of private insurance coverage meeting or exceeding minimum benefit standards, with co-insurance requirements ranging from 60% to 90%. Deductibles in the small-group market are capped at $2,000 per individual and $4,000 per family. Out-of-pocket requirements cannot exceed Health Savings Account limits, which will be reduced to $2,500 as of January 1, 2013. The exchanges must also offer a catastrophic-only plan to people less than 30 years of age or to individuals exempt from the law's mandate (requirement) that they obtain health care coverage.

Individuals who do not want to select a local private plan from the state exchanges will have the option of choosing from among multi-state private plans offering coverage similar to that enjoyed by members of Congress. As with all policies after 2014, none of these plans can exclude or charge more to anyone for a preexisting condition. Nor can they cap lifetime benefits or drop subscribers who become ill.

How To Buy ObamaCare

For coverage beginning January 1, 2014, a new way to buy insurance will be available in October of 2013. You will still be able to purchase insurance on your own directly from an insurance company or through a broker.

But you will also be able to use the new, state-based health insurance marketplaces, which are also called exchanges. There are two big advantages to using the online marketplace.

One, you can make side-by-side, "apples-to-apples" comparisons of all the available plans, and use an online calculator to find the best buy.

Two, you may qualify for an up-front discount in the form of a tax credit to help pay for your premiums, and you might also get help with your out-of-pocket costs.

Anyone without insurance through work can purchase private health insurance from the insurers participating in your state marketplace. And, you can also use it if your coverage at work costs you more than 9.5 percent of your income, or if your employer's plan does not meet the law's minimum standards.

The online marketplaces will be open for business starting October 1, 2013, offering coverage that starts January 1, 2014. States must decide whether to build their own or partner with the federal government. Some states will end up choosing to let the federal government run their online marketplaces..

How the Insurance Exchanges Work: Signing Up

Getting covered through President Barack Obama's health care law might feel like a combination of doing your taxes and making a big purchase that requires research.

You'll need accurate income information for your household, plus some understanding of how health insurance works, so you can get the financial assistance you qualify for and pick a health plan that's right for your needs.

The process involves federal agencies verifying your identity, citizenship and income, and you have to sign that you are providing truthful information, subject to perjury laws.

You heard it was going to be like buying airline tickets online? Not quite. But even if the process triggers some anxiety, it's not the government poking in your medical records, as "Obamacare" foes have suggested.

After state health insurance markets open Oct. 1, consumers can apply online, via a call center, in person or by mail. Trained helpers are supposed to be available, but there may not be enough of them.

The main steps are:

— Identify yourself and your family members.

— Provide current information on income, jobs and any available health insurance options.

— Learn how much financial assistance you're entitled to.

— Shop for a health plan and enroll.

Many people, ranging from lower-income workers to the solid middle class, will qualify for tax credits to help buy a private plan through the state markets. The government will send money directly to your insurer, and you'll make arrangements to pay any remaining premium.

The poor and near-poor will be steered to Medicaid in states that agree to expand that program.

Here's an overview of what to expect applying online, with tips:

Go to healthcare.gov and click on "Get Insurance." The site has links to every state market. You'll set up an account and password. You'll provide your contact information and the best way to reach you.

Tip — Treat your password like a bank account or credit card password. It's not a good idea to set it as "1234567."

Now you can tackle the actual application. You'll need birth dates and Social Security numbers for yourself and other family members listed on your federal tax return.

You'll also be asked if you're a citizen. Legal immigrants will need their immigration documents.

Tip — You don't have to plow through the entire application in one sitting. You can save your work and come back later.

Next, you'll be asked about income.

You may need your most recent tax return, pay stubs and details on other kinds of income, such as alimony, pensions and rents. You can still apply if you haven't filed a tax return. You'll also be asked about access to health insurance through your job. You may be required to take that insurance if available.

Your personal and income details will be routed through a new government entity called the data services hub, which will ping agencies like Social Security, Homeland Security and the Internal Revenue Service for verification. The feds will also rely on a major private credit reporting company to verify income and employment.

How smoothly all this works is one of the big unknowns. It could get tedious if discrepancies take time to resolve.

Tip — Provide the most accurate estimate of your expected income for 2014. Lowball the number, and you might see a smaller tax refund in 2015. Overestimate and you won't get as big a tax credit now.

If you're like most people, you'll be getting a tax credit to help pay your premiums. The credits are based on your income and keyed to the premium for a benchmark plan known as the "second-lowest cost silver plan" in your area.

With your tax credit, you can finally shop for insurance. Beware: you'll probably have to live with your decision until the next annual enrollment period.

You'll have up to four levels of coverage to consider: bronze, silver, gold and platinum. Plans at every "metal level" cover the same benefits and have a cap of $6,350 a year in out-of-pocket expenses for an individual, $12,700 for families.

Bronze plans generally have the lowest premiums, but cover only 60 percent of medical costs on average. Policyholders will pay the difference, up to the annual out of pocket cap. Platinum plans have the highest premiums, but cover 90 percent of costs. Young adults up to age 30 can pick a skinny "catastrophic" plan — but you can't use your tax credit on a catastrophic plan.

Tip — Make sure your doctors and hospitals are in the plan you pick. You may have to check the plan's own website, or call your doctor.

Tip — Your share of the premium could be lower — even zero — if you apply your tax credit to a bronze plan. It's because the credit is keyed to the cost of a silver plan, which is generally more expensive.

Tip — Check if you are eligible for "cost-sharing subsidies," in addition to your tax credit. Extra help with out-of-pocket costs is available to people with modest incomes. But only with a silver plan.

How the Insurance Exchanges Work: Choosing an Insurance Plan

After filling out your information you will be able to start shopping for health insurance. Like a car insurance website you will be able to compare plans, premium rates and benefits. Although all plans must include the 10 essential health benefits (see below), not all plans are created equal. Further down in the guide you will learn about the types of plans, their additional benefits, costs and your out of pocket costs.

The 10 Essential Health Benefits Required for All Plans Sold on the Exchange

Regardless of what tier of plan you purchase all plans must cover:

1. Ambulatory patient services
2. Emergency services
3. Hospitalization
4. Maternity and newborn care
5. Mental health and substance use disorder services, including behavioral health treatment
6. Prescription drugs
7. Rehabilitative and habilitative services and devices
8. Laboratory services
9. Preventive and wellness services and chronic disease management
10. Pediatric services, including oral and vision care

Types of Health Insurance Plans

There are a number of different tiers of plans available on your health insurance exchange. Plans range from bare bones "bronze" plans which cover 60% of pocket medical costs, to "platinum" plans which have greater coverage but come with a hefty 40% excise tax. The plans are as listed below:

NOTE: All cost sharing is of out of pocket costs. Please see ObamaCare health benefits for services that are covered at no out of pocket charge on all plans.

Bronze Plan: The bronze plan is the lowest cost plan available. It has the lowest premiums and in exchange has the lowest actuarial value. The actuarial value of a bronze plan is 60%. This means that 60% of medical costs are paid for by the insurance company, leaving the other 40% to be paid by you.

Silver Plan: The Silver plan is the second lowest cost plane, it has an actuarial value of 70%. This means that 70% of medical costs are paid for by the insurance company, leaving the other 30% to be paid by you. The Silver plan is the standard choice for most reasonably healthy families who historically use medical services.

Gold Plan: The Gold plan is the second most expensive plan, it has an actuarial value of 80%. This means that 80% of medical costs are paid for by the insurance company, leaving the other 20% to be paid by you

Platinum Plan: The Platinum plan is the plan with the highest premiums offered on the insurance exchange. The Platinum plan as an actuarial value of 90%. This means that 90% of medical costs are paid for by the insurance company, leaving the other 10% to be paid by you. This plan is suggested to those with high incomes and those in poor health. Although coverage is more expensive up front the 90% coverage of costs will help those who use medical services frequently.

Not every healthcare provider has to offer each tier of plan, however, all health insurance companies must offer at least one silver plan and one gold plan to consumers.

Tools Used For Shopping on the Affordable Insurance Exchange

In the past individuals and small businesses have paid higher premiums than larger firms since they lack the ability to pool risk and purchasing power. The Affordable Insurance Exchange provides consumers with a number of customer assistance tools for shopping on the exchange. Tools to access affordability and quality include comparisons of prices, quality, and physicians and hospital networks.

How to Calculate the Cost of Health Insurance

To get started you'll want to figure out what your budget is for health care this year. Affordable health insurance is defined as 8% of your income. Take your income for last year and find out if you can afford to pay 8%, if not find a number that you feel you can pay. Although insurance costs differ from State to State you can use this official cost calculator from the Cover California health insurance exchange (http://www.coveredca.com/calculating_the_cost.html) to get an idea of what your costs may be. Keep in mind that health, age and other factors can increase or decrease the cost of your insurance.

Source:

"How Does ObamaCare Work?" at http://obamacarefacts.com/howdoes-obamacare-work.php

CHAPTER SIX

Help Paying for Health Insurance

Probably the biggest concern for Americans is: When I'm required to buy health insurance, will I be able to afford it? From discounts and subsidies to specially designed plans for young adults, the heath-care law provides measures to help make insurance more affordable for people with low and moderate incomes.

Beginning in 2014, tax credits will be available to U.S. citizens and legal immigrants who purchase coverage in the new health insurance exchanges and who have income up to 400% of the federal poverty level ($43,320 for an individual or $88,200 for a family of four in 2009). To be eligible for the premium tax credits, individuals must not be eligible for public coverage—including Medicaid, the Children's Health Insurance Program, Medicare, or military coverage—and must not have access to health insurance through an employer. (There is an exception in cases when the employer plan does not cover at least 60 percent of covered benefits on average or the employee share of the premium exceeds 9.5% of the employee's income.)

The premium tax credits will be advanceable and refundable, meaning they will be available when an individual purchases coverage and will be available regardless of whether or not an individual owes any taxes. The premium tax credits will vary with income and are structured so that the premium an individual or family will have to pay will not exceed a specified percentage of income, ranging from 2% for those with incomes up to 133% of the poverty level (about $14,400 for an individual) to 9.5% for those with incomes between 300 and 400% of the poverty level ($32,490 to $43,320 for an individual).

In Addition To Premium Credits, Health Law Offers Some Consumers Help Paying Deductibles And Co-Pays

When people talk about health insurance affordability, they typically focus on premiums, the sticker price for a policy. For the plans being sold through the online health insurance marketplaces next year, much of the discussion has been on tax credits that can reduce the monthly premium for people with incomes up to 400 percent of the federal poverty level ($94,200 for a family of four in 2013).

But the Affordable Care Act also established another type of financial assistance for people who buy plans on the marketplaces, also known as exchanges. Cost-sharing subsidies can substantially reduce the deductibles, copayments, coinsurance and total out-of-pocket spending limits for people with incomes up to 250 percent of the federal poverty level ($58,875 for a family of four in 2013). Those reductions could be an important consideration for lower-income consumers when choosing their coverage.

"Particularly for people who have to utilize a high amount of services, the reduction in total out-of-pocket costs" can be important, says Dana Dzwonkowski, an expert on ACA implementation at the American Cancer Society's Cancer Action Network.

Cost-sharing reductions will be applied automatically for consumers who qualify based on their income, but only if they buy a silver-level plan, considered the benchmark under the law.

Silver plans are one of the four categories that will be sold on the exchanges, each named for a precious metal. Premiums for the plans will vary, and each will offer a different level of cost sharing for the consumer through deductibles and copayments, among other things. A silver plan will generally pay 70 percent of covered medical expenses, leaving the consumer responsible for 30 percent.

The insurer will typically cover 60 percent of expenses in a bronze plan, 80 percent in a gold plan and 90 percent in a platinum plan. All exchange plans will offer a similar package of comprehensive services that cover 10 so-called essential health benefits and cover certain types of preventive care at 100 percent.

The federal cost-sharing subsidies essentially increase the insurance company's share of covered benefits, resulting in reduced out-of-pocket spending for lower-income consumers. A family of four whose income is between 100 and 150 percent of the federal poverty level ($23,550 to $35,325) will be responsible for paying 6 percent of covered expenses out-of-pocket compared with the 30 percent that a family not getting subsidized coverage would owe in a silver plan. A family with an income between 150 and 200 percent of the poverty level ($35,325 to $47,100) will be responsible for 13 percent of expenses, and one with an income between 200 and 250 percent of the poverty level will be responsible for 27 percent ($47,100 to $58,875).

In addition, people who earn 250 percent of the federal poverty level or less will also have their maximum out-of-pocket spending capped at lower levels than will be the case for others who buy plans on the exchange. In 2014, the out-of-pocket limits for most plans will be $6,350 for an individual and $12,700 for a family. But people who qualify for cost-sharing subsidies will see their maximum out-of-pocket spending capped at $2,250 or $4,500 for single or family coverage, respectively, if their incomes are less than 200 percent of the poverty level, and $5,200 or $10,400 if their incomes are between 200 and 250 percent of poverty.

Insurers have some flexibility in how they structure their plans to meet cost-sharing reductions. But in states that will require plans to standardize deductibles, copayments and coinsurance amounts, it's possible to see how out-of-pocket costs may vary.

In California, for example, a standard silver plan will have a $2,000 deductible, a $6,400 maximum out-of-pocket limit and a $45 copayment for a primary care office visit. Someone whose income is between 150 and 200 of the poverty level, on the other hand, will have a silver plan with a $500 deductible, a $2,250 maximum out-of-pocket limit and $15 copays for primary care doctor visits.

Healthy people might be inclined to go with an exchange bronze plan or the catastrophic plan (a high-deductible plan available only to people under age 30 that will have lower premiums than a silver plan), figuring they won't need the cost-sharing assistance.

"It's an individual calculation," says Jennifer Tolbert, director of state health reform at the Kaiser Family Foundation. (KHN is an editorially independent program of the foundation.)

However, she says, services that aren't preventive in nature may be subject to a much higher deductible than in a silver plan--$5,000 in the case of the California bronze plan--and could result in significant cost sharing.

"And remember, those people are going to be getting pretty significant premium tax credits for the silver plan, which will bring the cost of premiums down quite a bit," she says.

Consumers should keep in mind, though, the cost-sharing subsidies apply to in-network expenses only. That may become an issue in some plans with limited provider networks.

"In the exchanges, a lot of insurers are going to narrower networks as a way to keep costs down," says Christine Monahan, a senior health policy analyst at Georgetown University's Center on Health Insurance Reforms. "If you go out of network, you could be subject to higher cost sharing and balance billing."

Sources: *Kaiser Health News*

CHAPTER SEVEN

The Medicaid Expansion

Medicaid was created by the Social Security Amendments of 1965 which added Title XIX to the Social Security Act. Medicaid was created as an entitlement program to help states provide medical coverage for low-income families and other categorically related individuals who meet eligibility requirements. Candidates include the blind, aged, disabled and pregnant women. In essence, Medicaid serves as the nation's primary source of health insurance coverage for low-income populations. Each state administers its own Medicaid program, establishes their own eligibility standards, determines the scope and types of services they will cover, and sets the rate of payment. Benefits vary from state to state, and because someone qualifies for Medicaid in one state, it does not mean they will qualify in another

To many, Medicaid is an enigma. The program's complexity surrounding who is eligible, what services are paid for, and how those services are reimbursed and delivered is one source of this confusion. Variability across State Medicaid programs is the rule, not the exception. In recent years, more and more States have implemented a variety of major program changes using special waiver authority. Income eligibility levels, services covered, and the method for and amount of reimbursement for services differ from State to State. Furthermore, Medicaid is a program that is targeted at individuals with low-income, but not all of the poor are eligible, and not all those covered are poor. For populations like children and families, primary and acute care often is delivered through managed care, while the elderly and disabled typically obtain such care on a fee-for-service basis.

The Affordable Care Act fills in current gaps in coverage for the poorest Americans by creating a minimum Medicaid income eligibility level across the country. Beginning in January 2014, individuals under 65 years of age with income below 133 percent of the federal poverty level (FPL) will be eligible for Medicaid. For the first time, low-income adults without children will be guaranteed coverage through Medicaid in every state without need for a waiver, and parents of children will be eligible at a uniform income level across all states. Medicaid and Children's Health Insurance Program (CHIP) eligibility and enrollment

Much be simpler and will be coordinated with the newly created Affordable Insurance Exchanges.

ObamaCare's Medicaid expansion expands Medicaid to the nation poorest in order cover nearly half of uninsured Americans. The law previously required states to cover their poorest or lose federal funding to Medicaid (federal funding covers 90-100% of the costs) until the Supreme Court ruling on ObamaCare. The law had said, prior to the Supreme Court hearing, those very low-income individuals (those under the 133% FLP line) including adults without dependent children. Even though Medicaid is a federal and state joint program the funding for low income individuals was covered 93% over the next decade by the federal government using tax payer money.

Medicaid Expansion Means, in all States, Individuals with annual incomes up to 133% of the federal poverty line -- currently, $14,856 or less -- are able to enroll. Right now eligibility differs from State to State. Unfortunately, when the NFIB took ObamaCare to the Supreme Court in order to repeal it, the Medicaid expansion requirement was overturned. National Federation of Independent Business *(NFIB) is an "independent" group that represents "small business". However they historically follow the Republican party line and fight against "entitlement" programs like ObamaCare's Medicaid Expansion that help the nations poorest and the majority of smaller businesses.*

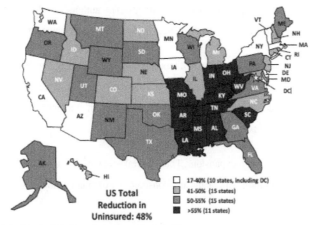

Figure ES-2
Reduction in Number of Uninsured Under ACA with All States Expanding Medicaid, 2022

US Total Reduction in Uninsured: 48%

- 17-40% (10 states, including DC)
- 41-50% (15 states)
- 50-55% (15 states)
- >55% (11 states)

Note: Includes effects of the Medicaid expansion and other provisions in the ACA.
Source: Urban Institute estimates prepared for the Kaiser Commission on Medicaid and the Uninsured, October 2012.

Now each state can decide whether or not they want to opt out of expanding coverage to their poorest with no penalty. The new ruling doesn't just hurt Medicaid and ObamaCare, it affects the tax payer by forcing us to pay for states that choose not to help their poorest.

Nearly ONE HALF of uninsured Americans were going to get their health Insurance under ObamaCare Medicaid reform by expanding coverage to the nation's poorest starting in 2014. Now states can opt out without losing federal funding.

What is "Wrong" With Medicaid

A number of academic studies over the years have illustrated that Medicaid patients have consistently had poor access to care and that Medicaid fails to meet important needs:

- A 1992 study in the *Journal of the American Medical Association* examined hospitalizations in Massachusetts and Maryland. The study found that Medicaid and uninsured patients were statistically more likely than privately insured patients to be hospitalized for avoidable conditions such as pneumonia and diabetes.
- A 2007 study in *Health Affairs* examined access to specialty services for patients who receive primary care from community health centers. The study found that Medicaid recipients have significantly more difficulty accessing specialty care than privately insured patients.
- A 2012 study in *Health Affairs* examined physicians' willingness to accept new patients. Using survey data from a nationally representative sample, the study found that nearly one-third of physicians nationwide will not accept new Medicaid patients. Doctors in smaller practices, as well as doctors in metropolitan areas, are among the least inclined to accept new Medicaid patients. The authors' results suggest that this reluctance may largely be a consequence of Medicaid's poor payment rates to doctors.

Given these findings in the peer-reviewed literature, it is not surprising that Medicaid patients often arrive at emergency rooms in poor, and in many cases, untreatable condition. In fact, research has shown that Medicaid and CHIP patients end up in emergency rooms even more frequently than uninsured patients.

Medicaid needs reform, not expansion. This federal–state health care program provides health care to over 60 million Americans and consumes a growing portion of state and federal budgets. Research shows a long history of Medicaid enrollees having worse access and outcomes than privately insured individuals. Due in part to low reimbursement, one in three doctors refuses to accept new Medicaid patients. Despite access issues, Medicaid spending continues to grow. In 2010, total federal and state spending on Medicaid exceeded $400 billion.

Instead of reforming Medicaid, the Patient Protection and Affordable Care Act (Obamacare) expands eligibility to *all* individuals earning less than 138 percent of the federal poverty level (FPL). The Medicaid program is already struggling to provide care to its core obligations—a diverse group of low-income children, disabled, pregnant women, and seniors. Adding more people further exacerbates Medicaid's underlying problems.

The expansion of Medicaid fuels a larger trend under Obamacare: government coverage supplanting private coverage. By 2021, 46 percent of all Americans will be dependent on the government for their health care. Of this group, 86.9 million will be on Medicaid/Children's Health Insurance Program (CHIP), followed by 64.3 million on Medicare and 23.4 million enrolled in government exchanges. This will push U.S. health care closer to a government model.

However, The ObamaCare Medicaid reforms that come with ObamaCare's Medicaid Expansion include raising the amount doctors get paid to the same level of Medicare (73%) and increasing payments to Medicaid programs that offer preventative services for free or at little cost. New free preventive services include tests for high blood pressure, diabetes, and high cholesterol; many cancer screenings including colonoscopies and mammograms; counseling to help people lose weight, quit smoking or reduce alcohol use; routine vaccinations; flu and pneumonia shots; and others.

The Temptation of Medicaid Expansion

Obamacare provides additional federal funding to the states for this new expansion population. Starting in 2014, the federal government would pick up 100 percent of the benefit costs for the newly eligible population for three years. Thereafter, this enhanced federal funding would gradually decline to 90 percent in 2020.

Obamacare also directed states to expand eligibility or risk forgoing *all* of their federal Medicaid dollars. The Supreme Court, however, ruled on behalf of 26 state plaintiffs that this "all-or-nothing" proposition was coercive. To rectify this, the Court essentially made the expansion optional, meaning that a state could reject the expansion but not lose its existing Medicaid funding.

Today, governors and state legislators are weighing this option as they develop their budgets for the coming year. Proponents use a variety of unrealistic arguments in support of the Medicaid expansion:

- **It provides states with an influx of new, generous federal revenue.** This will cause states to spend money that they otherwise would not have spent. Moreover, due to the structure of Obamacare, states will likely have to absorb many currently eligible but not enrolled individuals as well as those who lose their existing employer coverage. These effects would add to the cost.

- **It will result in savings as the cost of uncompensated care declines with expanded coverage.** Heritage data analysis shows that in the first few years, when federal funding is at its peak, states may see some savings. Over time, however, in the majority of states, Medicaid spending will accelerate and dwarf any projected uncompensated care savings. These savings are also contingent on states enacting legislation to further reduce uncompensated care funds (Disproportionate Share Hospital [DSH] payments) on top of the $18 billion of federal cuts enacted under Obamacare. Heritage analyst Ed Haislmaier predicts that "governors and state legislators should expect their state's hospitals and clinics to lobby them for more— not less—state funding to replace cuts in federal DSH payments." Finally, contrary to the theory that expanding Medicaid would cause the number of uninsured to decline and reduce the need for uncompensated care, a similar expansion in Maine found the opposite effect. In Maine, uncompensated care increased, and the number of uninsured in the targeted population (those below 100 percent of FPL) saw limited change.

- **Rejecting the expansion will mean that other states get more.** The federal share of Medicaid is based on a formula calculation and actual expenditures. Rejected funds do not go into a general fund for redistribution to other states. The fewer states that expand, the less the federal government spends. States that draw down on these new federal funds fuel the fiscal crisis in our country.

What if All States Moved Forward With Medicaid Expansion

If all States Move Forward with ObamaCare's Medicaid Expansion they will collectively pay $76 billion (a 3% increase) to insure up to 21.3 Million individuals who don't have access to health insurance (about half of the nations uninsured) over the next decade. Obviously those who have more to cover will have to spend more. Regardless of what a State Spends the Federal Government Covers 93% of the States Costs. State spending Increases are relatively small compared to what States would pay without ObamaCare or to the 26% increase that the federal government will pay towards Medicaid.

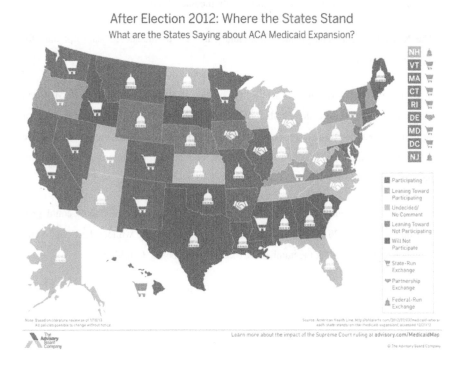

ObamaCare Medicaid Expansion Facts

• The federal government will pay a very high share of new Medicaid costs in all states. 100% of costs are cover for the first year. 90% of the spending is done by federal government moving forward.

• Increases in state spending are small compared to increases in coverage and federal revenues and relative to what states would have spent if reform had not been enacted

• ObamaCare Medicaid Expansion sets the eligibility level for Medicaid at 133% FLP, although there is a special deduction to income equal to five percentage points of the poverty level raising the effective eligibility level to 138% of poverty.

The legislation maintains existing income counting rules for the elderly and groups eligible through another program like foster care, low-income

Medicare beneficiaries and Supplemental Security Income (SSI))

• The NFIB helped to change the Affordable Care Act to include a "state opt out" for Medicaid Expansion.

• In combination with ObamaCare's other provisions, if all States participate in Medicaid expansion it would reduce the number of uninsured by 48%, relative to the number of uninsured without the ObamaCare. States with higher uninsured rates prior to the ObamaCare would see larger increases in Medicaid and bigger reductions in the uninsured, compared to states with lower pre-ObamaCare uninsured rates.

•If all states implement the expansion, an additional 21.3 million individuals could gain Medicaid coverage by 2022, a 41% increase compared to Medicaid without the ObamaCare. With many States opting out the number is expected to fall below 15 million.

• Medicaid Expansion covers those who are most likely to use emergency services costing hospitals tens of billions in unpaid hospital bills.

• States will spend little to nothing expanding Medicaid. For example it would cost the State of Florida about $5 a year per person to cover all uninsured below the 138% FLP.

• Low-income families and other Americans who would be eligible for Medicaid will fall between the cracks without expansion (as they do now). ObamaCare will most likely have to insure them in the ObamaCare health exchanges. This is projected to drive up the cost of insurance for all Americans by a great deal.

• Big Business backed groups like ALEC and the NFIB frequently suggest legislation that seeks to dismantle public programs at a state level. They tend to achieve this in Red states where they have the most pull. These states need Medicaid the most as they have the most low-income individuals falling through the cracks. They will also put a bigger burden on everyone else as it will cost more to insure their poorest on the exchange.

• If Medicaid Expansion is Opted out of by too many states it will greatly diminish the effectiveness and affordability of ObamaCare.

• The federal government will pay for most (90% - 100%) of the Medicaid expansion when it is implemented in 2014, but states would be required to pay for up to 10% percent of it by 2020.

• Some States, are saying that paying 0% - 10% of the Medicaid expansion as laid out under ObamaCare will cost them too much. While some States will pay more, the increase is very small (3% average increase in Medicaid Spending) even for the States who will pay the most.

• A Harvard case study found that states who had expanded their Medicaid programs from 2000 to 2005 improved health care for the state and saved thousands of lives.

• Some States are expected to save Billions from ObamaCare's Medicaid Expansion.

Which States Will Expand Medicaid under Medicaid Expansion?

Want to know which states will insure the 15 million Americans below the poverty line and which States will leave the rest of the 21.3 million uninsured behind? Find out which states support their state's poorest. Want more information on ObamaCare and Medicaid Expansion?

NOT PARTICIPATING (14 states)

- **Alabama***: Gov. Robert Bentley (R)
- **Florida*:** Gov. Rick Scott (R)
- **Georgia***: Gov. Nathan Deal (R)
- **Idaho***: Gov. C.L. Otter (R)

- **Iowa***: Gov. Terry Branstad (R)
- **Louisiana***: Gov. Bobby Jindal (R)
- **Maine***: Gov. Paul LePage (R)
- **Mississippi***: Gov. Phil Bryant (R)
- **North Carolina**: Gov. Pat McCrory (R)
- **Oklahoma**: Gov. Mary Fallin (R)
- **Pennsylvania***: Gov. Tom Corbett (R)
- **South Carolina***: Gov. Nikki Haley (R)
- **South Dakota**: Gov. Dennis Daugaard (R)
- **Texas***: Gov. Rick Perry (R)
- **Wisconsin***: Gov. Scott Walker (R)

LEANING TOWARD NOT PARTICIPATING (3 states)

- **Alaska*:** Gov. Sean Parnell (R)
- **Nebraska***: Gov. Dave Heineman (R)
- **Wyoming***: Gov. Matt Mead (R)

LEANING TOWARD PARTICIPATING (2 states)

- **Kentucky**: Gov. Steve Beshear (D
- **New York**: Gov. Andrew Cuomo (D)

PARTICIPATING (25 states and the District of Columbia)

- **Arizona***: Gov. Jan Brewer (R)
- **Arkansas:** Gov. Mike Beebe (D)
- **California**: Gov. Jerry Brown (D)
- **Colorado***: Gov. John Hickenlooper (D)
- **Connecticut**: Gov. Dannel Malloy (D)
- **Delaware**: Gov. Jack Markell (D)
- **District of Columbia**: D.C. Mayor Vincent Gray (D)
- **Hawaii**: Gov. Neil Abercrombie (D)
- **Illinois**: Gov. Pat Quinn (D)
- **Maryland**: Gov. Martin O'Malley (D

- **Massachusetts**: Gov. Deval Patrick (D)
- **Michigan***: Gov. Rick Snyder (R)
- **Minnesota**: Gov. Mark Dayton (D)
- **Missouri**: Gov. Jay Nixon (D)
- **Montana**: Gov.-elect Steve Bullock (D)
- **Nevada***: Gov. Brian Sandoval (R)
- **New Jersey**: Gov. Chris Christie (R)
- **New Hampshire:** Gov. Maggie Hassan (D)
- **New Mexico**: Gov. Susana Martinez (R)
- **North Dakota***: Gov. Jack Dalrymple (R)
- **Ohio***: Gov. John Kasich (R)
- **Oregon**: Gov. John Kitzhaber (D)
- **Rhode Island**: Gov. Lincoln Chaffee (I)
- **Vermont**: Gov. Peter Shumlin (D)

* indicates a state's participation in the multistate lawsuit against ACA

Who's Eligible Under the ObamaCare Medicaid Expansion

Medicaid is a joint federal-state program that provides health coverage or nursing home coverage to certain categories of low-asset people, including children, pregnant women, parents of eligible children, people with disabilities and elderly needing nursing home care. Medicaid was created to help low-asset people who fall into one of these eligibility categories "pay for some or all of their medical bills. Having limited assets is one of the primary requirements for Medicaid eligibility, but poverty alone does not qualify a person to receive Medicaid benefits unless they also fall into one of the defined eligibility categories. According to the CMS website, "Medicaid does not provide medical assistance for all poor persons. Even under the broadest provisions of the Federal statute (except for emergency services for certain persons), the Medicaid program does not provide health care services, even for very poor persons, unless they are in one of the designated eligibility groups.

There are a number of Medicaid eligibility categories; within each category there are requirements other than income that must be met. These other requirements include, but are not limited to, assets, age, pregnancy, disability, blindness, income and resources, and one's status as a U.S. citizen or a lawfully admitted immigrant.

Children

Medicaid and the Children's Health Insurance Program (CHIP) provide health coverage to more than 43 million children, including half of all low-income children in the United States. The federal government sets minimum guidelines for Medicaid eligibility but states can choose to expand coverage beyond the minimum threshold. All states have done so for children — the average CHIP income eligibility level for children is 241% of the Federal Poverty Level (FPL).

Eligibility

Most states have elected to provide Medicaid to children with family incomes above the minimum of 100% of the FPL, and all states have expanded coverage to children with higher incomes through the Children's Health Insurance Program (CHIP).

In general, children in families with incomes up to $44,700/year (for a family of four in 2011) are likely to be eligible for Medicaid or CHIP coverage. In many states, families with higher incomes can still qualify for coverage for their children. This includes children in mandatory Medicaid eligibility groups, which states must cover in order to participate in Medicaid, as well as children in optional eligibility groups that a state may elect to cover. All children from birth to age 6 with family incomes up to 133% ($29,700 for a family of four in 2011) and children age 6-18 with family incomes up to 100% ($22,350 for a family of four in 2011) are eligible for Medicaid. Other eligible children include infants born to women covered by Medicaid (known as "deemed newborns"), certain children in foster care or an adoption assistance program and certain children with disabilities.

Benefits

All children enrolled in Medicaid are entitled to the comprehensive set of health care services known as Early, Periodic Screening, Diagnosis and Treatment (EPSDT). CHIP also ensures a comprehensive set of benefits for children, but states have flexibility to design the benefit package.

Non-Disabled Adults

Medicaid provides health coverage to 11 million non-elderly low-income parents, other caretaker relatives, pregnant women, and other non-disabled adults. States provide coverage to parents/caretaker relatives who are in mandatory eligibility groups and optional eligibility groups.

Eligibility levels for parents/caretaker relatives vary across the country and there is currently no federal requirement that states provide coverage to non-pregnant adults without dependent children. The Affordable Care Act creates a national minimum eligibility standard of 133% of the federal poverty level (FPL), beginning in 2014, which will include coverage of most adults under age 65 at this income level.

Parents & Caretaker Relatives

Parents/caretaker relatives in low-income families with dependent children are eligible for coverage if their income meets minimum eligibility levels established for financial and medical assistance in 1996, which averages 41% of the FPL. (1996 was the year of enactment for welfare reform, which held in place guaranteed Medicaid eligibility for those receiving AFDC benefits at that time.) Parents are also eligible for Medicaid if they are medically needy or through Transitional Medical Assistance (TMA). States have the option to cover parents with incomes above the 1996 minimum levels and many states do so as mandatory or optional Medicaid state plan coverage or as part of an 1115 waiver program.

Adults without Dependent Children

There is currently no federal requirement that states provide health coverage to adults without dependent children. These adults qualify for Medicaid coverage only if they have a disability or are age 65 or older. However, about half of states provide some coverage through federal waivers or state-funded programs for non-disabled adults who have limited incomes but do not otherwise qualify for Medicaid.

Affordable Care Act Provides Eligibility for Most Low-Income Adults

In 2014, individuals under age 65 (including parents and adults without dependent children) with incomes below 133% of the FPL ($14,500 for an individual in 2011) will become eligible for Medicaid in every state. This change ends the longstanding coverage gap for low-income adults. States can choose to expand eligibility for adults prior to 2014, and several states have already done so.

Pregnant Women

Medicaid plays a key role in child and maternal health, financing 40% of all births in the United States. Medicaid coverage for pregnant women includes prenatal care through the pregnancy, labor, and delivery, and for 60 days postpartum as well as other pregnancy-related care.

Eligibility

States have the option to extend Medicaid coverage to pregnant women up to or over 185% and most states have done so. In addition, some states have medically needy programs, which allow pregnant women with incomes above the medically needy income threshold to spend down to eligibility if their health care expenses are sufficiently high.

Once eligibility is established, pregnant women remain eligible for Medicaid through the end of the calendar month in which the 60th day after the end of the pregnancy falls, regardless of any change in family income.

Infants born to pregnant women who are receiving Medicaid for the date of delivery are automatically eligible for Medicaid (known as "deemed newborns"). Medicaid eligibility continues until the child's first birthday and citizenship documentation is not required.

Benefits

Pregnant women receive care related to the pregnancy, labor, and delivery and any complications that may occur during pregnancy, as well as perinatal care for 60 days post partum. States have the option to provide pregnant women with full Medicaid coverage, or they may elect to limit coverage to certain pregnancy-related services.

Seniors & Medicare and Medicaid Enrollees

Medicaid provides health coverage to more than 4.6 million low-income seniors, nearly all of whom are also enrolled in Medicare. Medicaid also provides coverage to 3.7 million people with disabilities who are enrolled in Medicare. In total, 8.3 million people are "dually eligible" and enrolled in both Medicaid and Medicare, composing more than 17% of all Medicaid enrollees. Individuals who are enrolled in both Medicaid and Medicare, by federal statute, can be covered for both optional and mandatory categories.

What Medicaid Covers for Medicare Enrollees

Medicare has four basic forms of coverage:

Part A: Pays for hospitalization costs

Part B: Pays for physician services, lab and x-ray services, durable medical equipment, and outpatient and other services

Part C: Medicare Advantage Plan(like an HMO or PPO) offered by private companies approved by Medicare

Part D: Assists with the cost of prescription drugs

Medicare enrollees who have limited income and resources may get help paying for their premiums and out-of-pocket medical expenses from Medicaid (e.g. MSPs, QMBs, SLBs, and QIs). Medicaid also covers additional services beyond those provided under Medicare, including nursing facility care beyond the 100-day limit or skilled nursing facility care that Medicare covers, prescription drugs, eyeglasses, and hearing aids. Services covered by both programs are first paid by Medicare with Medicaid filling in the difference up to the state's payment limit.

Medicare and Medicaid Enrollee Category	Eligibility Level	Resource Standards	What Medicaid Pays for
Qualified Medicare Beneficiary (QMB)	100% FPL	$6,680/ individual, $10,020/ couple	Part A premiums, Part B premiums, deductibles/coinsurance/copayments
Specified Low-Income Medicare Beneficiary (SLMB)	120% FPL	$6,680/ individual,	Part B premiums only

		$10,020/ couple	
Qualified Individual (QI)	135% FPL	$6,680/ individual, $10,020/ couple	Part B premiums only
Qualified Disabled Working Individual (QDW)	200% FPL	$4,000/ individual, $6,000/ couple	Part A premiums only

Other Eligibility Groups

Medically Needy

Many states have what are called "medically needy programs", which are optional for states. Individuals with significant health needs, whose income is too high to otherwise qualify for Medicaid under other eligibility groups can still become eligible by "spending down" the amount of income that is above a particular state's medically needy income standard. Individuals spend down by incurring expenses for medical and remedial care. If once those incurred expenses are subtracted from the person's annual income and the person's income is at or below the state's medically needy income standard, the person can be eligible for Medicaid. The Medicaid program then pays the cost of services that exceed what the individual had to incur in the way of expenses in order to become eligible.

In addition to states with medically needy programs, states that determine Medicaid eligibility of the aged, blind, and disabled using more restrictive eligibility criteria than are used by the Supplemental Security Income (SSI) program (known as 209(b) states) also allow individuals to spend down their excess income to the state's categorically needy income standard. 209(b) states must allow a spenddown to their categorically needy income standard even if the state also has a medically needy program.

Thirty-six states and the District of Columbia use spenddown programs, either as medically needy programs or as 209(b) states.

Breast & Cervical Cancer Prevention and Treatment Program

States can choose to provide Medicaid coverage to certain groups of women who are in need of treatment for breast and cervical cancer. Women are screened through the Centers for Disease Control and Prevention's (CDC) National Breast and Cervical Cancer Early Detection Program.

In order for a woman to be eligible for Medicaid under this option, she must:

- Have been screened for and found to have breast or cervical cancer, including precancerous conditions, through the National Breast and Cervical Cancer Early Detection Program (NBCCEDP)
- Be determined to need treatment for breast or cervical cancer;
- Be under age 65; and
- Be uninsured and otherwise not eligible for Medicaid.

Tuberculosis (TB)

States can choose to provide Medicaid financing for coverage of tuberculosis-related services to low-income individuals who are infected with TB. This eligibility group serves individuals who are not otherwise eligible for Medicaid based on the traditional eligibility categories.

Services available to people who are eligible under the optional TB group include the following TB-related services:

- Prescribed drugs;
- Physician's services and services (including outpatient hospital services, rural health clinic services, and federally qualified health center services);
- Laboratory and X-ray services (including those to confirm the presence of infection);
- Clinic services and federally qualified health center services;
- Case management services; and

- Services (other than room and board) designed to encourage completion of regimens of prescribed drugs by outpatients, including services to directly observe the intake of prescribed drugs.

Why the ObamaCare Medicaid Expansion Matters

About half of our nations uninsured are in danger of losing coverage on a state level. Letting states Opt out of ObamaCare's Medicaid drives the costs up for the rest of Americans who choose to help their poorest and drives up our taxes and the cost of healthcare. On a human level these low-income individuals won't have access to healthcare and under the current law they won't receive help in the online market place under a certain income (this makes health insurance affordable for the rest of us).

Most of all on a "business" level hospitals and healthcare as a whole will suffer since they will still have to care for these individuals via emergency uncompensated care which will shift even more costs back on us.

CHAPTER EIGHT

Changes for Small and Large Businesses

Are you a small business owner? Are you afraid of the coming changes under Obamacare, or do you think you will you benefit from them? When the Affordable Care Act goes into full effect in 2014, businesses can expect the following changes:

1. Small Businesses (<25 Employees)

Health care reform, also known as the Affordable Care Act (ACA), will have important effects on small businesses with less than 25 full-time employees. Some changes are easy to implement, simply requiring employers to take compliance action, but several provisions in the new law pose more strategic issues for employers. This means businesses must make some key decisions regarding health care benefits for their employees, followed by both appropriate implementation actions and adequate communications. Key provisions outlined by the U.S. Small Business Administration include:

Small Business Tax Credits : *If your business employs fewer than 25 full-time equivalent workers with average annual wages not exceeding $50,000, your business may be eligible for the Small Business Health Care Tax Credit. Starting January 1, 2014, small business tax credits will expand to 50 percent of a small business' premium costs for two consecutive years.*

Small Business Health Option Program (SHOP) Marketplace: Small employers* are eligible to participate in the SHOP Marketplace in 2014. Eligible employers that choose to offer insurance through the SHOP Marketplace are required to offer SHOP insurance coverage to all full-time employees. Starting in 2015, the SHOP Marketplace will provide a premium aggregation service and will send a single invoice to the employer. The SHOP Marketplace will offer two models:

1. **Employer-choice** *(available in 2014)*: The employer selects the plans, and employees can then choose from the employer's selected options.
2. **Employee-choice** *(delayed until 2015)*: The employer selects an actuarial value level, and employees can select from any available plans at the employer's selected level through the SHOP Marketplace.

*In the case of plan years beginning before January 1, 2016, a State may elect to define small employer by substituting "50 employees" for "100 employees".

New Summary of Benefits

Major medical insurers began sending all benefits enrollees and applicants a new summary of benefits booklet and coverage notice to explain their benefit plans and coverage. If your business has a self-funded plan, you will be required to provide the new summary for annual enrollment periods on or after September 23, 2012, as well as all other enrollments for plan years beginning on or after January 1, 2013. [2]

Medical Loss Ratio Rebate Distribution

Major medical insurers that do not meet new medical loss ratio (MLR) requirements are required to issue rebates to policyholders by August 1st every year (beginning in 2012). In most cases, it is the employer's responsibility to distribute the participant portion within three months of receiving the rebate. The details on distribution depend on the type of plan offered (e.g., church plan, ERISA, etc.) [3]

Flexible Spending Account (FSA) Limits:

For cafeteria plan years beginning on and after Jan. 1, 2013, employer-sponsored cafeteria plans must limit employee annual salary reduction contributions to health flexible spending arrangements to $2,500. The $2,500 limit applies to employee participants on a plan-year basis, and will be indexed for cost-of-living adjustments for future plan years. [4]

Note: The limit does not apply to certain employer non-elective health FSA contributions, or to any contributions or amounts available for reimbursement under other types of FSAs (such as a dependent care FSA), health savings accounts (HSAs), health reimbursement arrangements (HRAs), or to salary reduction contributions to cafeteria plans used to pay an employee's share of health coverage premiums.

Additional Medicare Withholding on Wages

A 0.9 percent additional Medicare tax goes into effect starting in 2013, raising the Medicare tax rate for certain earners from 1.45 percent to 2.35 percent. The additional Medicare tax applies to an individual's wages, Railroad Retirement Tax Act compensation, and self-employment income that exceeds a threshold amount based on the individual's filing status ($250,000 for married taxpayers who file jointly, $125,000 for married taxpayers who file separately, and $200,000 for all other taxpayers). It is paid solely by employees and does not have to be matched by employers; however, the employer is responsible for withholding the additional Medicare tax from wages or compensation paid to an employee in excess of $200,000 in a calendar year. [5]

New Medicare Assessment on Net Investment Income

Starting in 2013, a new 3.8 percent Net Investment Income Tax will be applied to individuals, estates and trust with income with net investment income and modified adjusted gross income above certain thresholds ($250,000 for married taxpayers who file jointly, $125,000 for married taxpayers who file separately, and $200,000 for all other taxpayers). Investment income may include interest, dividends, capital gains, rental and royalty income, non-qualified annuities, income from businesses involved in trading of financial instruments or commodities, and businesses that are passive activities to the taxpayer. [6]

Waiting Period Limits

Beginning January 1, 2014, the ACA restricts waiting periods to a maximum of 90 days. [7]

Required Contribution to the Temporary Reinsurance Program

During the first three years post reform (2014–2016), a temporary reinsurance program for the individual insurance market will be funded by a required contribution from all group major medical plans. The per capita amount is paid for each enrollee by the insurer or third-party administrators on behalf of self-funded plans. [8]

Employer Wellness Incentives

Health care reform increases the maximum permissible reward under a health-contingent wellness program from 20 percent to 30 percent of the cost of health coverage, and also increases the maximum reward to as much as 50 percent for programs designed to prevent or reduce tobacco use. Generally, a health-contingent wellness program requires individuals to meet a specific health standard to gain a reward. Examples include: a reward for not using or decreasing use of tobacco, or a reward for achieving a specified cholesterol level or weight. [9]

Health Insurance Coverage Reporting

Self-insured employers must report information to the IRS on the employees receiving coverage, dates of coverage and other information the Department of Health and Human Services (HHS) may require. They must also identify the employer, the employer-paid portion of the premium and other information HHS may require with respect to the small employer tax credit. Statements are to be provided annually to employees by January 31st. The annual reporting begins in 2016 for the 2015 plan year.

2. Small Employers (<50 Employees)

Health care reform, also known as the Affordable Care Act (ACA), will have important effects on small employers with less than 50 full-time employees in 2013. Some changes are easy to implement, simply requiring employers to take compliance action, but several provisions in the new law pose more strategic issues for employers. This means businesses must make some key decisions regarding health care benefits for their employees, followed by both appropriate implementation actions and adequate communications. Key provisions outlined by the U.S. Small Business Administration include:

Small Business Health Option Program Marketplace: Small employers* are eligible to participate in the SHOP Marketplace in 2014. Eligible employers that choose to offer insurance through the SHOP Marketplace are required to offer SHOP insurance coverage to all full-time employees. Starting in 2015, the SHOP Marketplace will provide a premium aggregation service and will send a single invoice to the employer, as well as offer two models:

1. **Employer-choice** *(available in 2014)*: The employer selects the plans, and employees can then choose from the employer's selected options.

2. **Employee-choice** *(delayed until 2015)*: The employer selects an actuarial value level, and employees can select from any available plans at the employer's selected metal level on the SHOP Marketplace.

*In the case of plan years beginning before January 1, 2016, a State may elect to define small employer by substituting "50 employees" for "100 employees".

New Summary of Benefits

Major medical insurers began sending all benefits enrollees and applicants a new summary of benefits booklet and coverage notice to explain their benefit plans and coverage. If your business has a self-funded plan, you will be required to provide the new summary for annual enrollment periods on or after September 23, 2012, as well as all other enrollments for plan years beginning on or after January 1, 2013. [1]

Medical Loss Ratio rebate distribution

Major medical insurers that do not meet new medical loss ratio (MLR) requirements are required to issue rebates to policyholders by August 1 [st] every year (beginning in 2012). In most cases, it is the employer's responsibility to distribute the participant portion within three months of receiving the rebate. The details on distribution depend on the type of plan offered (e.g., church plan, ERISA, etc.). [2]

Flexible Spending Account (FSA) Limits: For cafeteria plan years beginning on and after Jan. 1, 2013, employer-sponsored cafeteria plans must limit employee annual salary reduction contributions to health flexible spending arrangements to $2,500. The $2,500 limit applies to employee participants on a plan-year basis, and will be indexed for cost-of-living adjustments for future plan years. [3]

Additional Medicare Withholding on Wages

A 0.9 percent additional Medicare tax goes into effect starting in 2013, raising the Medicare tax rate for certain earners from 1.45 percent to 2.35 percent. The additional Medicare tax applies to an individual's wages, Railroad Retirement Tax Act compensation, and self-employment income that exceeds a threshold amount based on the individual's filing status ($250,000 for married taxpayers who file jointly, $125,000 for married taxpayers who file separately, and $200,000 for all other taxpayers). It is paid solely by employees and does not have to be matched by employers; however, the employer is responsible for withholding the additional Medicare tax from wages or compensation paid to an employee in excess of $200,000 in a calendar year. [4]

New Medicare Assessment on Net Investment Income

Starting in 2013, a new 3.8 percent Net Investment Income Tax will be applied to individuals, estates and trust with income with net investment income and modified adjusted gross income above certain thresholds ($250,000 for married taxpayers who file jointly, $125,000 for married taxpayers who file separately, and $200,000 for all other taxpayers). Investment income may include interest, dividends, capital gains, rental and royalty income, non-qualified annuities, income from businesses involved in trading of financial instruments or commodities, and businesses that are passive activities to the taxpayer. [5]

Waiting Period Limits

Beginning January 1, 2014, the ACA restricts waiting periods to a maximum of 90 days. [6]

Required contribution to the temporary reinsurance program

During the first three years post reform (2014–2016), a temporary reinsurance program for the individual insurance market will be funded by a required contribution from all group major medical plans. The per capita amount is paid for each enrollee by the insurer or third-party administrators on behalf of self-funded plans. [7]

Employer Wellness Incentives

Health care reform increases the maximum permissible reward under a health-contingent wellness program from 20 percent to 30 percent of the cost of health coverage, and also increases the maximum reward to as much as 50 percent for programs designed to prevent or reduce tobacco use. Generally, a health-contingent wellness program requires individuals to meet a specific health standard to gain a reward. Examples include: a reward for not using or decreasing use of tobacco, or a reward for achieving a specified cholesterol level or weight. [8]

Health Insurance Coverage Reporting

Self-insured employers must report information to the IRS on the employees receiving coverage, dates of coverage and other information the Department of Health and Human Services (HHS) may require. They must also identify the employer, the employer-paid portion of the premium and other information HHS may require with respect to the small employer tax credit. Statements are to be provided annually to employees by January 31st. The annual reporting begins in 2016 for the 2015 plan year.

3. *Large Employers (50+ Employees)*

Health care reform, also known as the Affordable Care Act (ACA), will have important effects on employers with 50 or more full-time employees. Some changes are easy to implement, simply requiring employers to take compliance action, but several provisions in the new law pose more strategic issues for employers. This means businesses must make some key decisions regarding health care benefits for their employees, followed by both appropriate implementation actions and adequate communications. Key provisions outlined by the U.S. Small Business Administration include:

Shared Responsibility/Employer Mandate (i.e. "Pay or Play")

Starting in 2015, employers with 50 or more full-time employees will be subject to a shared responsibility payment if at least one employee obtains a premium tax credit or cost-share reduction through the Health Insurance Marketplace. [1] The penalty calculation varies based on whether or not the employer offers affordable, minimum essential coverage to substantially all full-time employees and dependents. [2]

New Summary of Benefits

Major medical insurers began sending all benefits enrollees and applicants a new summary of benefits booklet and coverage notice to explain their benefit plans and coverage. If your business has a self-funded plan, you will be required to provide the new summary for annual enrollment periods on or after September 23, 2012, as well as all other enrollments for plan years beginning on or after January 1, 2013. [3]

Medical Loss Ratio rebate distribution

Major medical insurers that do not meet new medical loss ratio (MLR) requirements are required to issue rebates to policyholders by August1 [st] every year (began in 2012). In most cases, it is the employer's responsibility to distribute the participant portion within three months of receiving the rebate. The details on distribution depend on the type of plan offered (e.g., church plan, ERISA, etc.). [4]

W-2 Reporting

To help show how much an employer contributes toward an employee's health care coverage, employers that issued 250 or more W-2's in the prior year are required to report the total aggregate cost of major medical health benefits and certain pre-tax funded supplemental health coverage provided to each employee on their 2012 W-2 Forms. This information will be reported in Box 12, using Code DD. The reporting is for informational purposes only and has no tax impact to the employer. Reporting is optional for employers who file fewer than 250 W-2s until further guidance is issued by the IRS. [5]

Limits on Flexible Spending Account (FSA)

For cafeteria plan years beginning on and after Jan. 1, 2013, employer-sponsored cafeteria plans must limit employee annual salary reduction contributions to health flexible spending arrangements to $2,500. The $2,500 limit applies to employee participants on a plan-year basis, and will be indexed for cost-of-living adjustments for future plan years. [6]

Note: The limit does not apply to certain employer non-elective health FSA contributions, or to any contributions or amounts available for reimbursement under other types of FSAs (such as a dependent care FSA), health savings accounts (HSAs), health reimbursement arrangements (HRAs), or to salary reduction contributions to cafeteria plans used to pay an employee's share of health coverage premiums.

Additional Medicare Withholding on Wages

A 0.9 percent additional Medicare tax goes into effect starting in 2013, raising the Medicare tax rate for certain earners from 1.45 percent to 2.35 percent. The additional Medicare tax applies to an individual's wages, Railroad Retirement Tax Act compensation, and self-employment income that exceeds a threshold amount based on the individual's filing status ($250,000 for married taxpayers who file jointly, $125,000 for married taxpayers who file separately, and $200,000 for all other taxpayers). It is paid solely by employees and does not have to be matched by employers; however, the employer is responsible for withholding the additional Medicare tax from wages or compensation paid to an employee in excess of $200,000 in a calendar year. [7]

New Medicare Assessment on Net Investment Income

Starting in 2013, a new 3.8 percent Net Investment Income Tax will be applied to individuals, estates and trust with income with net investment income and modified adjusted gross income above certain thresholds ($250,000 for married taxpayers who file jointly, $125,000 for married taxpayers who file separately, and $200,000 for all other taxpayers). Investment income may include interest, dividends, capital gains, rental and royalty income, non-qualified annuities, income from businesses involved in trading of financial instruments or commodities, and businesses that are passive activities to the taxpayer. [8]

Waiting Period Limits

Beginning January 1, 2014, the ACA restricts waiting periods to a maximum of 90 days. [8]

During the first three years post reform (2014–2016), a temporary reinsurance program for the individual insurance market will be funded by a required contribution from all group major medical plans. The per capita amount is paid for each enrollee by the insurer or third-party administrators on behalf of self-funded plans. [10]

Employer Wellness Incentives

Health care reform increases the maximum permissible reward under a health-contingent wellness program from 20 percent to 30 percent of the cost of health coverage, and also increases the maximum reward to as much as 50 percent for programs designed to prevent or reduce tobacco use. Generally, a health-contingent wellness program requires individuals to meet a specific health standard to gain a reward. Examples include: a reward for not using or decreasing use of tobacco, or a reward for achieving a specified cholesterol level or weight. [11]

Health Insurance Coverage Reporting

Employers subject to shared responsibility standards and self-insured employers must report information to the IRS on the employee receiving coverage, dates of coverage, the employer paid portion of the premium, and other information the Department of Health and Human Services (HHS) may require. Statements are to be provided annually to employees by January 31st. The annual reporting begins in 2016 for the 2015 plan year.

How to Take Advantage of the Small Business Health Care Tax Credit

Small Businesses can apply for tax breaks of up to 35% (25% for non-profits) of the cost of their employees premiums if they have fewer than 25 full-time employees. Through 2013, to qualify for a small business tax credit of up to 35% (up to 25% for non-profits) of your premium contributions, you must have all of these criteria:

- Fewer than 25 full-time equivalent employees

- Pay average annual wages below $50,000
- Contribute 50% or more toward your employees' self-only health insurance premiums

Beginning in 2014, this tax credit increases to 50% (35% for non-profits) and will be available to small businesses who meet the criteria listed above and who purchase coverage through the new Small Business Health Options Program (SHOP) Marketplaces (also known as Exchanges). This enhanced credit can be claimed for any two consecutive taxable years beginning in 2014 (or beginning in a later year) through the SHOP.

While any business meeting the above standards may be eligible to receive a tax credit of up to 35% (25% for non-profits), the Small Business Health Care Tax Credit works on a sliding scale and is specifically targeted for those businesses with low- and moderate-income workers.

For this reason, to qualify for the maximum small business tax credit, you must contribute at least 50% toward your employees' self-only premium costs and meet the following two standards:

- 10 or fewer full-time employees
- Annual average wages at or below $25,000

Once you've determined that you qualify for the credit, your tax professional and the IRS can help guide you through the necessary steps to claim the credit which include:

- Check with your tax professional; even if you are a small business employer who did not owe tax during the year, you may be able to carry the credit back or forward to other tax years. And if you are a tax-exempt employer, you may be eligible for a refundable credit.

- Use **Form 8941** Credit for Small Employer Health Insurance Premiums, to calculate the credit. It's also important to know that eligible small employers can still claim a business expense deduction for the remainder of their premium contributions.

- This is a federal tax credit. Check to see if your state has additional health care tax credits available to small employers.

More information about the Small Business Health Care Tax Credit is available from the IRS at *http://www.irs.gov/uac/Small-Business-Health-Care-Tax-Credit-for-Small-Employers*

The Small Business Health Options Program (SHOP)

Starting in 2014, individuals and small businesses will have the same affordable insurance choices as Members of Congress and will be able to purchase private health insurance through State-based competitive marketplaces called Affordable Insurance Exchanges. An Exchange is a State-based competitive health insurance marketplace where people and small businesses can shop for and buy affordable private health insurance. By 2014, every State will have an Exchange tailored to its local insurance market. Tax credits will be available for many individuals, families and businesses to help them purchase coverage in the Exchanges.

Open enrollment for individual and small business health insurance exchanges begins Oct. 1, 2013. Businesses with up to 100 employees will be eligible, although States can limit participation to businesses with up to 50 employees until 2016. "Exchanges are probably the most important provision of health-care reform for small businesses because they will help lower costs and improve choice of plans." Businesses will use a specific part of the exchange called SHOP– that offers small businesses and their employees new choices. Through the SHOP, employers can offer employees a variety of Qualified Health Plans (QHPs), and their employees can choose the plans that fit their needs and their budget.

SHOPs can help your small business by:

Simplifying Choices: SHOPs will provide side-by-side comparisons of Qualified Health Plans, their benefits, premiums, and quality. Under the Affordable Care Act, premiums will no longer be based on the employees' health or medical history as they now are in many States. Instead, premiums can vary only based on the ages and smoking histories of employees. Some States may opt for even stronger consumer protections. Employees cannot be excluded from a plan or denied plan benefits because of a pre-existing health condition.

Expanding Employee Options: SHOPs will enable you to offer your employees a choice of Qualified Health Plans from several insurers, much as large employers can. All plans will cover essential health benefits like those covered by a typical employer health plan. Benefits will be offered in four "tiers" based on the amount of coverage that they provide. SHOP will provide information to you and your workers to allow you to compare benefits across health plans.

Preserving Employer Control: You will be able to decide whether and when to participate in SHOP. You will be able to choose your own level of contribution toward your employees' coverage, and make a single monthly payment via SHOP rather than to multiple plans.

Lowering your costs: A SHOP will reduce the burden and costs of enrolling your employees in small group plans, and give you many of the cost advantages and choices enjoyed by large businesses today. SHOP will do the work for you of finding qualified health plans, getting information on their price and benefits, enrolling your employees, and consolidating billing. You choose what share of the premium cost to cover. And, depending on the Exchange in your State, you choose which qualified health plans to offer your employees.

You'll also have exclusive access to an expanded Small Business Healthcare Tax Credit. This tax credit covers as much as 50% of the employer contribution toward premium costs for eligible employers who have low- to moderate-wage workers. When you get insurance through the SHOP, it makes it easy for you take advantage of other tax breaks too including the chance for you and your employees to use pre-tax dollars to make your premium payments.

What other benefits does a SHOP have?

Besides lowering your costs and increasing your employees' plan choice, SHOPs can:

- Help you and your employees compare your insurance options available through the SHOP using an Exchange website. This website will help you compare qualified health plans, their benefits, pricing, and quality of different plan options and give employees a clear, simple enrollment form.
- Provide personalized support to answer your questions and help you choose the best coverage option for yourself and your employees.
- Protect your business by ensuring that all qualified health plans meet basic minimum Federal and State standards, such as standards of quality and provider choice.

What's the difference between a SHOP and the current small group insurance market?

Unlike the current marketplace, a SHOP will:

- Guarantee small businesses a choice of qualified health plans to offer to employees.
- Require health insurers to give you detailed information about the prices, benefits, and quality of their qualified health plans, in a format that lets you easily make "apples to apples" comparisons between qualified health plans.
- Post quality information and the price for each qualified plan on the Exchange website, along with the results of consumer satisfaction surveys.
- Consolidate billing so you can offer workers a choice without the hassle of contracting with multiple insurers.

How can I get access to the SHOP for my small business?

SHOPs are a program of the new Affordable Insurance Exchanges. States have flexibility in whether and how to structure Exchanges that meet local needs. Exchanges ensure that the health insurance plans offered to participants meet minimum standards to protect consumers and choices.

If I'm not a small business owner or employee, can I purchase health insurance in the SHOP?

No, only small business owners and their employees can buy health insurance through a SHOP. However, individuals without affordable employer coverage have access to an individual Exchange that offers the same kind of competitive marketplaces as the SHOP.

Deciding Where to Go From Here

These are the basics of the Obamacare effects on small and large businesses like yours so, whether you're up and running now, or you plan to be soon, it pays to familiarize yourself with the act so that you can make sure you have a strong understanding of what it entails and how you will be affected by it.

Going forward, health insurance may be something that you will have to factor into your business planning, so it makes sense to conduct a full and thorough financial analysis in order to gauge the viability of health insurance within your organization. Consider three essential questions to help make more informed decisions for your workforce and your business.

Essential Question 1: Should I offer employer provided coverage or not?

Most business leaders agree health benefits offer employees peace of mind and protection. Businesses large and small rely on health benefits to provide a unique competitive-edge in the battle to attract and retain talented workers.

Whether your business is a long-time employee benefits provider, or you are considering employer-sponsored benefits for the first time, with deadlines looming for health care reform now is the time to look at the size of your business, employee demographics, and the cost advantages and disadvantages of providing health coverage.

- **Tip for small businesses:** Employer-sponsored benefits may offer you a cost-effective way to boost employee compensation. Although employers with less than 50 full-time equivalents (FTEs) **will not** be penalized for not providing a health plan, still many small businesses realize health benefits are an important part of an employee's total compensation package.

    If you currently offer health insurance to employees, some individuals may be eligible for a tax-subsidy to purchase individual coverage through the federal and state Health Insurance Marketplace (employees with a household income between 100 and 400 percent of the federal poverty level [FPL]). In which case, it may be cheaper for them to purchase coverage through the Marketplace. On the other hand, employees not eligible for a tax-subsidy could benefit from employer-provided coverage as opposed to purchasing individual coverage through the Health Insurance Marketplace. The 2013 Aflac WorkForces Report revealed 78 percent of employees say their benefits package is important to their job satisfaction, and 65 percent say it is important to their loyalty to their employer.

78% of employees say their benefits package affects their job satisfaction, and 65% say it affects their loyalty to their employer. [1]

- **Tip for mid-to-large sized businesses:** Starting in 2015, employers with more than 50 FTEs may be subject to penalties if they do not provide affordable and minimum value employer-sponsored health insurance [2]. The majority of employers (88 percent) say they will continue to offer health benefits to active employees in 2014 [3]. As you consider whether to provide coverage, keep in mind that an employer's contribution to a health benefits plan is tax-deductible, whereas the $2,000 - $3,000 penalty for not providing affordable coverage is not.

The majority of employers (88%) say they will continue to offer health benefits to active employees in 2014. [3]

Essential Question 2: How much can my business afford to spend?

As you consider offering employer-sponsored health insurance, it is important to assess the amount your business can invest in workforce benefits.

- **If your business already offers employer-sponsored benefits:** You most likely have a good idea of how much your business can afford to pay. Take into consideration projected increases in health care costs, and your potential eligibility to take advantage of the Small Business Health Options Program (SHOP) in 2014. If your business is mid-to-large sized and rising costs are a concern, consider a private marketplace that offers fixed contribution options to help control costs.

- **If you are considering offering these benefits for the first time:** Discuss your options with your benefits consultant or broker to help weigh the costs. For instance, in 2013, health care costs are expected to increase per employee by 5.3 percent (0.6 percent lower than in 2012). [3] You can use cost estimates to determine approximately how much it will cost per-employee, as well as potential penalties for not providing employee health coverage. Additionally, you can estimate your eligibility for small business tax credits to help defray the costs associated with health care coverage through the Health Insurance Marketplace.

In 2013, health care costs are expected to increase per employee by 5.3% (0.6% lower than in 2012) The average expected un-subsidized costs of individual coverage is projected at $11,607 ($8,911 employer share, and $2,696 employee share). [3]

Essential Question 3: Which strategy will I choose?

Employee benefits are a key indicator of employee satisfaction, retention and productivity. In fact, the 2013 Aflac WorkForces Report revealed that workers who are extremely or very satisfied with their benefits program are three times more likely to stay with their employer than those workers who are dissatisfied with their benefits program. [1] With many options to choose from, including traditional insurance, self-insurance, HMO, PPO, affordable coverage, or a combination of options, take time to determine your business strategy. A few strategies to consider include:

- **Adjust current health plan:** Talk with your broker or benefits consultant to understand how your current benefits work within new ACA standards. You may find that your benefits already meet or exceed federal standards, and can actually capitalize on going above and beyond to help protect workforce health and wellbeing. As you assess your current plan, keep in mind that employees may be eligible for tax subsidies through the Health Insurance Marketplace if their required contribution to employer-sponsored health insurance exceeds 9.5 percent of the employee's annual gross income or the plan pays less than 60% of covered health expenses. [4]

- **Health Insurance Marketplace:** The Health Insurance Marketplace (also called an exchange) is expected to offer competitive benefits options to small businesses and individuals. Additionally, small businesses participating in the Marketplace may be eligible for a tax credit of up to 50% of their premium payments if they have 25 or fewer full-time employees whose average annual wages are no more than $50,000. [5]

    While it is still too early to tell exactly how competitive the Marketplace will be, tax credits coupled with options in the Marketplace may help your business to provide cost-effective workplace benefits. If you are considering shifting employees to the Marketplace, you may save on health care costs that could be allocated to supplemental benefits or employee salaries to provide increased value to your employees.

- **Self-funded model:** Self-funded health care insurance plans offer an alternative to traditional health care models. In a self-funding model, the company is responsible for covering all claims in the health care plan, but because these plans are excluded from some requirements of the ACA, employers can save costs related to premium taxes and state insurance regulations.

  Self-funded plans tend to shift additional costs to employees, especially when an employer has a workforce with significant health care needs. Companies may also need to consider adding adequate stop-loss coverage to accommodate for annual and lifetime dollar limit restrictions. Still, these plans are becoming increasingly popular with small businesses and can help to reduce and manage employee health care costs, while still delivering the health coverage that their workforce demands.

- **Defined contribution model:** In a defined contribution model, employers give their employees a fixed amount of money and a list of health insurance options for employees to pick and choose. This helps employers to keep costs predictable, while also offering employees the option to "buy-up" to more robust insurance coverage. Since these programs require employees to make more informed decisions about health care, it will be increasingly important they understand how an employer contribution works, and how to choose supplemental options to augment out-of-pocket costs.

Sources:

www.obamacarefacts.com

Meredith K. Olafson, "How to Take Advantage of the Small Business Health Care Tax Credit" found at http://www.sba.gov/community/blogs/community-blogs/health-care-business-pulse/how-take-advantage-small-business-healthreform

American Family Life Assurance Company of Columbus

References

[1] 2013 Aflac WorkForces Report, a study conducted by Research Now on behalf of Aflac, January 7 – 24, 2013.

[2] U.S. Department of Treasury (2013). Continuing to implement the ACA in a careful, thoughtful manner. Accessed July 2, 2013, from http://www.treasury.gov/connect/blog/Pages/Continuing-to-Implement-the-ACA-in-a-Careful-Thoughtful-Manner-.aspx.

[3] Towers Watson, 2012 Health Care Trends Survey, accessed on November 8, 2012, from towerswatson.com/en-US/ Insights/IC-Types/Survey-Research-Results/2012/10/health-care-changes-ahead-survey-report   .

[4] Congressional Research Service (2010). Summary of Potential Employer Penalties under the Patient Protection and Affordable Care Act (ACA), accessed on November 9, 2012, from ncsl.org/documents/health/EmployerPenalties.pdf.

[5] The White House, Small Business Health Care Tax Credit, accessed on November 8, 2012, from whitehouse.gov/healthreform/small-business/tax-credit.

CHAPTER NINE

The Price Tag

Obamacare contains some tax provisions that are in effect and more that will be implemented during the next several years, but which ObamaCare taxes will you actually pay; how will the new taxes in Obamacare, tax breaks and tax credits affect you, your family and your business? The following is a list of provisions for which the IRS has issued proposed and/or final guidance:

ObamaCare Income Tax Penalty For Not Having Insurance

Starting in 2014, most people will have to have insurance or pay a "penalty deducted from your taxable income". For individuals, penalty starts at $95 a year, or up to 1% of income, whichever is greater, and rise to $695, or 2.5% of income, by 2016.

For families the tax will be $2,085 or 2.5% percent of household income, whichever is greater. The requirement can be waived for several reasons, including financial hardship or religious beliefs. If the tax would exceed 8% of your income you are exempt, also some religious groups are exempt. That tax cannot exceed the cost of a "bronze plan" bought on the exchange.

While some states, including Alabama, Wyoming and Montana, have passed laws to block the requirement to carry health insurance, those provisions do not override federal law.

Net Investment Income Tax

A new Net Investment Income Tax goes into effect starting in 2013. The 3.8 percent Net Investment Income Tax applies to individuals, estates and trusts that have certain investment income above certain threshold amounts.

1. What is the Net Investment Income Tax (NIIT)?

The Net Investment Income Tax is imposed by section 1411 of the Internal Revenue Code (IRC). The NIIT applies at a rate of 3.8 percent to certain net investment income of individuals, estates and trusts that have income above the statutory threshold amounts.

2. When does the Net Investment Income Tax take effect?

The Net Investment Income Tax goes into effect on Jan. 1, 2013. The NIIT will affect income tax returns of individuals, estates and trusts for their first tax year beginning on (or after) Jan. 1, 2013. It will not affect income tax returns for the 2012 taxable year that will be filed in 2013.

Who Owes the Net Investment Income Tax

3. What individuals are subject to the Net Investment Income Tax?

Individuals will owe the tax if they have Net Investment Income and also have modified adjusted gross income over the following thresholds:

Filing Status	Threshold Amount
Married filing jointly	$250,000
Married filing separately	$125,000
Single	$200,000
Head of household (with qualifying person)	$200,000
Qualifying widow(er) with dependent child	$250,000

Taxpayers should be aware that these threshold amounts are not indexed for inflation.

If you are an individual that is exempt from Medicare taxes, you still may be subject to the Net Investment Income Tax if you have Net Investment Income and also have modified adjusted gross income over the applicable thresholds.

4. What individuals are not subject to the Net Investment Income Tax?

Nonresident Aliens (NRAs) are not subject to the Net Investment Income Tax. If an NRA is married to a U.S. citizen or resident and has made, or is planning to make, an election under IRC section 6013(g) to be treated as a resident alien for purposes of filing as Married Filing Jointly, the proposed regulations provide these couples special rules and a corresponding IRC section 6013(g) election for the NIIT.

5. What Estates and Trusts are subject to the Net Investment Income Tax?

Estates and Trusts will be subject to the Net Investment Income Tax if they have undistributed Net Investment Income and also have adjusted gross income over the dollar amount at which the highest tax bracket for an estate or trust begins for such taxable year (for tax year 2012, this threshold amount is $11,650). There are special computational rules for certain unique types of trusts, such a Charitable Remainder Trusts and Electing Small Business Trusts, which can be found in the proposed regulations (see # 19 below).

6. What Trusts are not subject to the Net Investment Income Tax?

The following trusts are not subject to the Net Investment Income Tax:

a. Trusts that are exempt from income taxes imposed by Subtitle A of the Internal Revenue Code (e.g., charitable trusts and qualified retirement plan trusts exempt from tax under IRC section 501, and Charitable Remainder Trusts exempt from tax under IRC section 664).
b. A trust in which all of the unexpired interests are devoted to one or more of the purposes described in IRC section 170(c)(2)(B).
c. Trusts that are classified as "grantor trusts" under IRC sections 671-679.
d. Trusts that are not classified as "trusts" for federal income tax purposes (e.g., Real Estate Investment Trusts and Common Trust Funds).

What is Included in Net Investment Income

7. What is included in Net Investment Income?

In general, investment income includes, but is not limited to: interest, dividends, capital gains, rental and royalty income, non-qualified annuities, income from businesses involved in trading of financial instruments or commodities, and businesses that are passive activities to the taxpayer (within the meaning of IRC section 469). To calculate your Net Investment Income, your investment income is reduced by certain expenses properly allocable to the income (see #12 below).

8. What are some common types of income that are not Net Investment Income?

Wages, unemployment compensation; operating income from a nonpassive business, Social Security Benefits, alimony, tax-exempt interest, self-employment income, Alaska Permanent Fund Dividends (see Rev. Rul. 90-56, 1990-2 CB 102) and distributions from certain Qualified Plans (those described in sections 401(a), 403(a), 403(b), 408, 408A, or 457(b)).

9. What kinds of gains are included in Net Investment Income?

To the extent that gains are not otherwise offset by capital losses, the following gains are common examples of items taken into account in computing Net Investment Income:

a. Gains from the sale of stocks, bonds, and mutual funds.
b. Capital gain distributions from mutual funds.
c. Gain from the sale of investment real estate (including gain from the sale of a second home that is not a primary residence).

Gains from the sale of interests in partnerships and S corporations (to the extent you were a passive owner).

10. Does this tax apply to gain on the sale of a personal residence?

The Net Investment Income Tax will not apply to any amount of gain that is excluded from gross income for regular income tax purposes. The pre-existing statutory exclusion in IRC section 121 exempts the first $250,000 ($500,000 in the case of a married couple) of gain recognized on the sale of a principal residence from gross income for regular income tax purposes and, thus, from the NIIT.

Example 1: A, a single filer, earns $210,000 in wages and sells his principal residence that he has owned and resided in for the last 10 years for $420,000. A's cost basis in the home is $200,000. A's realized gain on the sale is $220,000. Under IRC section 121, A may exclude up to $250,000 of gain on the sale. Because this gain is excluded for regular income tax purposes, it is also excluded for purposes of determining Net Investment Income. In this example, the Net Investment Income Tax does not apply to the gain from the sale of A's home.

Example 2: B and C, a married couple filing jointly, sell their principal residence that they have owned and resided in for the last 10 years for $1.3 million. B and C's cost basis in the home is $700,000. B and C's realized gain on the sale is $600,000. The recognized gain subject to regular income taxes is $100,000 ($600,000 realized gain less the $500,000 IRC section 121 exclusion). B and C have $125,000 of other Net Investment Income, which brings B and C's total Net Investment Income to $225,000. B and C's modified adjusted gross income is $300,000 and exceeds the threshold amount of $250,000 by $50,000. B and C are subject to NIIT on the lesser of $225,000 (B's Net Investment Income) or $50,000 (the amount B and C's modified adjusted gross income exceeds the $250,000 married filing jointly threshold). B and C owe Net Investment Income Tax of $1,900 ($50,000 X 3.8%).

Example 3: D, a single filer, earns $45,000 in wages and sells her principal residence that she has owned and resided in for the last 10 years for $1 million. D's cost basis in the home is $600,000. D's realized gain on the sale is $400,000. The recognized gain subject to regular income taxes is $150,000 ($400,000 realized gain less the $250,000 IRC section 121 exclusion), which is also Net Investment Income. D's modified adjusted gross income is $195,000. Since D's modified adjusted gross income is below the threshold amount of $200,000, D does not owe any Net Investment Income Tax.

11. Does Net Investment Income include interest, dividends and capital gains of my children that I report on my Form 1040 using Form 8814?

The amounts of Net Investment Income that are included on your Form 1040 by reason of Form 8814 are included in calculating your Net Investment Income. However, the calculation of your Net Investment Income does not include (a) amounts excluded from your Form 1040 due to the threshold amounts on Form 8814 and (b) amounts attributable to Alaska Permanent Fund Dividends.

12. What investment expenses are deductible in computing NII?

In order to arrive at Net Investment Income, Gross Investment Income (items described in items 7-11 above) is reduced by deductions that are properly allocable to items of Gross Investment Income. Examples of properly allocable deductions include investment interest expense, investment advisory and brokerage fees, expenses related to rental and royalty income, and state and local income taxes properly allocable to items included in Net Investment Income.

13. Will I have to pay both the 3.8% Net Investment Income Tax and the additional .9% Medicare tax?

You may be subject to both taxes, but not on the same type of income.

The 0.9% Additional Medicare Tax applies to individuals' wages, compensation and self-employment income over certain thresholds, but it does not apply to income items included in Net Investment Income.

How the Net Investment Income Tax is Reported and Paid

14. If I am subject to the Net Investment Income Tax, how will I report and pay the tax?

For individuals, the tax will be reported on, and paid with, the Form 1040. For Estates and Trusts, the tax will be reported on, and paid with, the Form 1041.

15. Is the Net Investment Income Tax subject to the estimated tax provisions?

The Net Investment Income Tax is subject to the estimated tax provisions. Individuals, estates, and trusts that expect to be subject to the tax in 2013 or thereafter should adjust their income tax withholding or estimated payments to account for the tax increase in order to avoid underpayment penalties.

16. Does the tax have to be withheld from wages?

No, but you may request that additional income tax be withheld from your wages.

Examples of the Calculation of the Net Investment Income Tax

17. How does a Single taxpayer with income less than the statutory threshold calculate the Net Investment Income Tax?

Taxpayer, a single filer, has wages of $180,000 and $15,000 of dividends and capital gains. Taxpayer's modified adjusted gross income is $195,000, which is less than the $200,000 statutory threshold. Taxpayer is not subject to the Net Investment Income Tax.

18. How does a Single taxpayer with income greater than the statutory threshold calculate the Net Investment Income Tax?

Taxpayer, a single filer, has $180,000 of wages. Taxpayer also received $90,000 from a passive partnership interest, which is considered Net Investment Income. Taxpayer's modified adjusted gross income is $270,000.

Taxpayer's modified adjusted gross income exceeds the threshold of $200,000 for single taxpayers by $70,000. Taxpayer's Net Investment Income is $90,000.

The Net Investment Income Tax is based on the lesser of $70,000 (the amount that Taxpayer's modified adjusted gross income exceeds the $200,000 threshold) or $90,000 (Taxpayer's Net Investment Income). Taxpayer owes NIIT of $2,660 ($70,000 x 3.8%).

Additional Information

19. Other than these FAQs, where can I find additional information about the Net Investment Income Tax?

Find it in the full text of the proposed regulations, request for comments, and information on the public hearing.

20. The proposed regulations are proposed to be effective for tax years beginning after Dec. 31, 2013, but Net Investment Income Tax goes into effect on Jan. 1, 2013. May I rely on the regulations for guidance on the Net Investment Income Tax during 2013?

Taxpayers may rely on the proposed regulations for purposes of compliance with section 1411 until the effective date of the final regulations. To the extent the proposed regulations provide taxpayers with the ability to make an election, taxpayers may make the election provided that the election is made in the manner described in the proposed regulation. Any election made in reliance on the proposed regulations will be in effect for the year of the election, and will remain in effect for subsequent taxable years. However, if final regulations provide for the same or a similar election, taxpayers who opt not to make an election in reliance on the proposed regulations will not be precluded from making that election pursuant to the final regulations.

Additional Medicare Tax

A new Additional Medicare Tax goes into effect starting in 2013. The 0.9 percent Additional Medicare Tax applies to an individual's wages, Railroad Retirement Tax Act compensation, and self-employment income that exceeds a threshold amount based on the individual's filing status. The threshold amounts are $250,000 for married taxpayers who file jointly, $125,000 for married taxpayers who file separately, and $200,000 for all other taxpayers. An employer is responsible for withholding the Additional Medicare Tax from wages or compensation it pays to an employee in excess of $200,000 in a calendar year.

BASIC FAQs

1. **When does Additional Medicare Tax start?**
   Additional Medicare Tax applies to wages and compensation above a threshold amount received after December 31, 2012 and to self-employment income above a threshold amount received in taxable years beginning after December 31, 2012.

2. **What is the rate of Additional Medicare Tax?**
   The rate is 0.9 percent.

3. **When are individuals liable for Additional Medicare Tax?**
   An individual is liable for Additional Medicare Tax if the individual's wages,

compensation, or self-employment income (together with that of his or her spouse if filing a joint return) exceed the threshold amount for the individual's filing status:

Filing Status	Threshold Amount
Married filing jointly	$250,000
Married filing separately	$125,000
Single	$200,000
Head of household (with qualifying person)	$200,000
Qualifying widow(er) with dependent child	$200,000

4.
5. **What wages are subject to Additional Medicare Tax?**
   All wages that are currently subject to Medicare Tax are subject to Additional Medicare Tax if they are paid in excess of the applicable threshold for an individual's filing status. For more information on what wages are subject to Medicare Tax, see the chart, Special Rules for Various Types of Services and Payments, in section 15 of Publication 15, (Circular E), Employer's Tax Guide.

6. **What Railroad Retirement Tax Act (RRTA) compensation is subject to Additional Medicare Tax?**
   All RRTA compensation that is currently subject to Medicare Tax is subject to Additional Medicare Tax if it is paid in excess of the applicable threshold for an individual's filing status. All FAQs that discuss the application of the Additional Medicare Tax to wages also apply to RRTA compensation, unless otherwise indicated.

7. **Are nonresident aliens and U.S. citizens living abroad subject to Additional Medicare Tax?**
   There are no special rules for nonresident aliens and U.S. citizens living abroad for purposes of this provision. Wages, other compensation, and self-employment income that are subject to Medicare tax will also be subject to Additional Medicare Tax if in excess of the applicable threshold.

8. **Additional Medicare Tax goes into effect for taxable years beginning after December 31, 2012; however, the proposed regulations (REG-130074-11) are not effective until after the notice and comment period has ended and final regulations have been published in the Federal Register. How will this affect**

Additional Medicare Tax requirements for employers, employees, or self-employed?

Additional Medicare Tax applies to wages, compensation, and self-employment income received in tax years beginning after December 31, 2012. Taxpayers must comply with the law as of that date. With regard to specific matters discussed in the proposed regulations, taxpayers may rely on the proposed regulations for tax periods beginning before the date that the final regulations are published in the Federal Register. If any requirements change in the final regulations, taxpayers will only be responsible for complying with the new requirements from the effective date of the final regulations.

INDIVIDUAL FAQs

8. **Will Additional Medicare Tax be withheld from an individual's wages?**
An employer must withhold Additional Medicare Tax from wages it pays to an individual in excess of $200,000 in a calendar year, without regard to the individual's filing status or wages paid by another employer. An individual may owe more than the amount withheld by the employer, depending on the individual's filing status, wages, compensation, and self-employment income. In that case, the individual should make estimated tax payments and/or request additional income tax withholding using Form W-4, Employee's Withholding Allowance Certificate.

9. **Will Additional Medicare Tax be withheld from an individual's compensation subject to Railroad Retirement Tax Act (RRTA) taxes?**
An employer must withhold Additional Medicare Tax from RRTA compensation it pays to an individual in excess of $200,000 in a calendar year without regard to the individual's filing status or compensation paid by another employer. An individual may owe more than the amount withheld by the employer, depending on the individual's filing status, wages, compensation, and self-employment income. In that case, the individual should make estimated tax payments and/or request additional income tax withholding using Form W-4, Employee's Withholding Allowance Certificate.

10. **Can I request additional withholding specifically for Additional Medicare Tax?**
No. However, if you anticipate liability for Additional Medicare Tax, you may request that your employer withhold an additional amount of income tax withholding on Form W-4. The additional income tax withholding will be applied against your taxes shown

on your individual income tax return (Form 1040), including any Additional Medicare Tax liability.

11. **Will I need to make estimated tax payments for Additional Medicare Tax?**
If you anticipate that you will owe Additional Medicare Tax but will not satisfy the liability through Additional Medicare Tax withholding and did not request additional income tax withholding using Form W-4, you may need to make estimated tax payments. You should consider your estimated total tax liability in light of your wages, other compensation, and self-employment income, and the applicable threshold for your filing status when determining whether estimated tax payments are necessary.

12. **Does an individual who makes estimated tax payments to pay an expected liability for Additional Medicare Tax need to identify the payments as specifically for this tax?**
No. An individual cannot designate any estimated payments specifically for Additional Medicare Tax. Any estimated tax payments that an individual makes will apply to any and all tax liabilities on the individual income tax return (Form 1040), including any Additional Medicare Tax liability.

13. **Will individuals calculate Additional Medicare Tax liability on their income tax returns?**
Yes. Individuals liable for Additional Medicare Tax will calculate Additional Medicare Tax liability on their individual income tax returns (Form 1040). Individuals will also report Additional Medicare Tax withheld by their employers on their individual tax returns. Any Additional Medicare Tax withheld by an employer will be applied against all taxes shown on an individual's income tax return, including any Additional Medicare Tax liability.

14. **Will an individual owe Additional Medicare Tax on all wages, compensation, and/or self-employment income or just the wages, compensation, and/or self-employment income in excess of the threshold for the individual's filing status?**
An individual will owe Additional Medicare Tax on wages, compensation, and/or self-employment income (and that of the individual's spouse if married filing jointly) that exceed the applicable threshold for the individual's filing status. For married persons filing jointly the threshold is $250,000, for married persons filing separately the threshold is $125,000, and for all others the threshold is $200,000.

15. **If my employer withholds Additional Medicare Tax from my wages in excess of $200,000, but I won't owe the tax because my spouse and I file a joint return and we won't meet the $250,000 threshold for joint filers, can I ask my employer to stop withholding Additional Medicare Tax?**

No. Your employer must withhold Additional Medicare Tax on wages it pays to you in excess of $200,000 in a calendar year. Your employer cannot honor a request to cease withholding Additional Medicare Tax if it is required to withhold it. You will claim credit for any withheld Additional Medicare Tax against the total tax liability shown on your individual income tax return (Form 1040).

16. **What should I do if I have two jobs and neither employer withholds Additional Medicare Tax, but the sum of my wages exceeds the threshold at which I will owe the tax?**

If you anticipate that you will owe Additional Medicare Tax but will not satisfy the liability through Additional Medicare Tax withholding (for example, because you will not be paid wages in excess of $200,000 in a calendar year by an employer), you should make estimated tax payments and/or request additional income tax withholding using Form W-4. For information on making estimated tax payments and requesting an additional amount be withheld from each paycheck, see Publication 505, Tax Withholding and Estimated Tax.

17. **Are wages that are not paid in cash, such as fringe benefits, subject to Additional Medicare Tax?**
Yes, the value of taxable wages not paid in cash, such as noncash fringe benefits, are subject to Additional Medicare Tax, if, in combination with other wages, they exceed the individual's applicable threshold. Noncash wages are subject to Additional Medicare Tax withholding, if, in combination with other wages paid by the employer, they exceed the $200,000 withholding threshold.

18. **Are   tips   subject   to   Additional   Medicare   Tax?**
Yes, tips are subject to Additional Medicare Tax, if, in combination with other wages, they exceed the individual's applicable threshold. Tips are subject to Additional

117

Medicare Tax withholding, if, in combination with other wages paid by the employer, they exceed the $200,000 withholding threshold.

19. **How do individuals calculate Additional Medicare Tax if they have wages subject to Federal Insurance Contributions Act (FICA) tax and self-employment income subject to Self-Employment Contributions Act (SECA) tax?**

Individuals with wages subject to FICA tax and self-employment income subject to SECA tax calculate their liabilities for Additional Medicare Tax in three steps:

Step 1 Calculate Additional Medicare Tax on any wages in excess of the applicable threshold for the filing status, without regard to whether any tax was withheld.

Step 2 Reduce the applicable threshold for the filing status by the total amount of Medicare wages received - but not below zero.

Step 3 Calculate Additional Medicare Tax on any self-employment income in excess of the reduced threshold.

Example 1: C, a single filer, has $130,000 in wages and $145,000 in self-employment income.
   1. C's wages are not in excess of the $200,000 threshold for single filers, so C is not liable for Additional Medicare Tax on these wages.
   2. Before calculating the Additional Medicare Tax on self-employment income, the $200,000 threshold for single filers is reduced by C's $130,000 in wages, resulting in a reduced self-employment income threshold of $70,000.
   3. C is liable to pay Additional Medicare Tax on $75,000 of self-employment income ($145,000 in self-employment income minus the reduced threshold of $70,000).

Example 2: D and E are married and file jointly. D has $150,000 in wages and E has $175,000 in self-employment income.

1.
   1. D's wages are not in excess of the $250,000 threshold for joint filers, so D and E are not liable for Additional Medicare Tax on D's wages.

118

2. Before calculating the Additional Medicare Tax on E's self-employment income, the $250,000 threshold for joint filers is reduced by D's $150,000 in wages resulting in a reduced self-employment income threshold of $100,000.

3. D and E are liable to pay Additional Medicare Tax on $75,000 of self-employment income ($175,000 in self-employment income minus the reduced threshold of $100,000).

i.   Example 3: F, who is married and files separately, has $175,000 in wages and $50,000 in self-employment income.

   1. F is liable to pay Additional Medicare Tax on $50,000 of his wages ($175,000 minus the $125,000 threshold for married persons who file separately).

   2. Before calculating the Additional Medicare Tax on self-employment income, the $125,000 threshold for married persons who file separately is reduced by F's $175,000 in wages to $0 (reduced, but not below zero).

   3. F is liable to pay Additional Medicare Tax on $50,000 of self-employment income ($50,000 in self-employment income minus the reduced threshold of $0).

   4. In total, F is liable to pay Additional Medicare Tax on $100,000 ($50,000 of his wages and $50,000 of his self-employment income).

Example 4: G, a head of household filer, has $225,000 in wages and $50,000 in self-employment income. G's employer withheld Additional Medicare Tax on $25,000 ($225,000 minus the $200,000 withholding threshold).

   5. G is liable to pay Additional Medicare Tax on $25,000 of her wages ($225,000 minus the $200,000 threshold for head of household filers).

   6. Before calculating the Additional Medicare Tax on self-employment income, the $200,000 threshold for head of household filers is reduced by G's $225,000 in wages to $0 (reduced, but not below zero).

   7. G is liable to pay Additional Medicare Tax on $50,000 of self-employment income ($50,000 in self-employment income minus the reduced threshold of $0).

   8. In total, G is liable to pay Additional Medicare Tax on $75,000 ($25,000 of her wages and $50,000 of her self-employment income).

119

9. The Additional Medicare Tax withheld by G's employer will be applied against all taxes shown on her individual income tax return, including any Additional Medicare Tax liability.

20. **How do individuals calculate Additional Medicare Tax if they have compensation subject to Railroad Retirement Tax Act (RRTA) taxes and wages subject to Federal Insurance Contributions Act (FICA) tax?** Compensation subject to RRTA taxes and wages subject to FICA tax are not combined to determine Additional Medicare Tax liability. The threshold applicable to an individual's filing status is applied separately to each of these categories of income.

Example: J and K, are married and file jointly. J has $190,000 in wages subject to Medicare tax and K has $150,000 in compensation subject to RRTA taxes. J and K do not combine their wages and RRTA compensation to determine whether they are in excess of the $250,000 threshold for a joint return. J and K are not liable to pay Additional Medicare Tax because J's wages are not in excess of the $250,000 threshold and K's RRTA compensation is not in excess of the $250,000 threshold.

21. **How do individuals calculate Additional Medicare Tax if they have compensation subject to Railroad Retirement Tax Act (RRTA) taxes and self-employment income subject to Self-Employment Contributions Act (SECA) tax?**

The threshold applicable to an individual's filing status is applied separately to RRTA compensation and self-employment income. In calculating Additional Medicare Tax on self-employment income, an individual does not reduce the applicable threshold for the taxpayer's filing status by the total amount of RRTA compensation. Example: F and G are married and file jointly. F has $160,000 in self-employment income and G has $140,000 in compensation subject to RRTA taxes. The $140,000 of RRTA compensation does not reduce the threshold at which Additional Medicare Tax applies to self-employment income. F and G are not liable to pay Additional Medicare Tax because F's self-employment income is not in excess of the $250,000 threshold and G's RRTA compensation is not in excess of the $250,000 threshold.

22. **Will I also owe net investment income tax on my income that is subject to Additional Medicare Tax?**
No. The new tax imposed by section 1411 on an individual's net investment income is

not applicable to FICA wages, RRTA compensation, or self-employment income. Thus, an individual will not owe net investment income tax on these categories of income, regardless of the taxpayer's filing status.

EMPLOYER and PAYROLL SERVICE PROVIDER FAQs

23. **When must an employer withhold Additional Medicare Tax?**
The statute requires an employer to withhold Additional Medicare Tax on wages it pays to an employee in excess of $200,000 in a calendar year, beginning January 1, 2013. An employer has this withholding obligation even though an employee may not be liable for Additional Medicare Tax because, for example, the employee's wages together with that of his or her spouse do not exceed the $250,000 threshold for joint return filers. Any withheld Additional Medicare Tax will be credited against the total tax liability shown on the individual's income tax return (Form 1040).

24. **Is an employer liable for Additional Medicare Tax even if it does not withhold it from an employee's wages?**
An employer that does not deduct and withhold Additional Medicare Tax as required is liable for the tax unless the tax that it failed to withhold from the employee's wages is paid by the employee. Even if not liable for the tax, an employer that does not meet its withholding, deposit, reporting, and payment responsibilities for Additional Medicare Tax may be subject to all applicable penalties.

25. **Is an employer required to notify an employee when it begins withholding Additional Medicare Tax?**
No. There is no requirement that an employer notify its employee.

26. **Is there an "employer match" for Additional Medicare Tax (as there is with the regular Medicare tax)?**
No. There is no employer match for Additional Medicare Tax.

27. **May an employee request additional withholding specifically for Additional Medicare Tax?**

No. However, an employee who anticipates liability for Additional Medicare Tax may request that his or her employer withhold an additional amount of income tax withholding on Form W-4. This additional income tax withholding will be applied

121

against all taxes shown on the individual's income tax return (Form 1040), including any Additional Medicare Tax liability.

28. **If an employee's annual Medicare wages are expected to be over $200,000, will an employer withhold Additional Medicare Tax from the beginning of the year or only after Medicare wages are actually paid in excess of $200,000 year-to-date?**

An employer is required to begin withholding Additional Medicare Tax in the pay period in which it pays wages in excess of $200,000 to an employee.

29. **If a single payment of wages to an employee exceeds the $200,000 withholding threshold, will an employer withhold Additional Medicare Tax on the entire payment?**

No. Additional Medicare Tax withholding applies only to wages paid to an employee that are in excess of $200,000 in a calendar year. Withholding rules for this tax are different than the income tax withholding rules for supplemental wages in excess of $1,000,000 as explained in Publication 15, section 7. Example: M received $180,000 in wages through November 30, 2013. On December 1, 2013, M's employer paid her a bonus of $50,000. M's employer is required to withhold Additional Medicare Tax on $30,000 of the $50,000 bonus and may not withhold Additional Medicare Tax on the other $20,000. M's employer also must withhold Additional Medicare Tax on any other wages paid in December 2013.

30. **I have two employees who are married to each other. Each earns $150,000, so I know that their combined wages will exceed the threshold applicable to married couples that file jointly. Do I need to withhold Additional Medicare tax?**

No. An employer should not combine wages it pays to two employees to determine whether to withhold Additional Medicare Tax. An employer is required to withhold Additional Medicare Tax only when it pays wages in excess of $200,000 in a calendar year to an employee.

31. **What should an employer do if an employee receives wages that are not paid in cash, such as taxable fringe benefits, from which Additional Medicare Tax cannot be withheld?**

If an employee receives wages from an employer in excess of $200,000 and the wages include taxable noncash fringe benefits, the employer calculates wages for purposes of withholding Additional Medicare Tax in the same way that it calculates wages for withholding the existing Medicare tax. The employer is required to withhold Additional Medicare Tax on total wages, including taxable noncash fringe benefits, in excess of $200,000. The value of taxable noncash fringe benefits must be included in wages and the employer must withhold the applicable Additional Medicare Tax and deposit the tax under the rules for employment tax withholding and deposits that apply to taxable noncash fringe benefits. Additional information on how to withhold tax on taxable noncash fringe benefits is available in Publication 15 (Circular E), section 5, and Publication 15-B, section 4.

32. **If an employee receives tips and other wages in excess of $200,000 in the calendar year, how is Additional Medicare Tax paid on the tips?** To the extent that tips and other wages exceed $200,000, an employer applies the same withholding rules for Additional Medicare Tax as it does currently for Medicare tax. An employer withholds Additional Medicare Tax on the employee's reported tips from wages it pays to the employee.

If the employee does not receive enough wages for the employer to withhold all the taxes that the employee owes, including Additional Medicare Tax, the employee may give the employer money to pay the rest of the taxes. If the employee does not give the employer money to pay the taxes, then the employer makes a current period adjustment on Form 941, Employer's QUARTERLY Federal Tax Return (or the employer's applicable employment tax return), to reflect any uncollected employee social security, Medicare, or Additional Medicare Tax on reported tips. However, unlike the uncollected portion of the regular (1.45%) Medicare tax, the uncollected Additional Medicare Tax is not reported in box 12 of Form W-2 with code B.

The employee may need to make estimated tax payments to cover any shortage. More information about this process of giving an employer money for taxes is available in Publication 531, Reporting Tip Income.

33. **If a former employee receives group-term life insurance coverage in excess of $50,000 and the cost of the coverage, in combination with other wages, exceeds $200,000, how does an employer report Additional Medicare Tax on this?** The imputed cost of coverage in excess of $50,000 is subject to social security and

Medicare taxes, and to the extent that, in combination with other wages, it exceeds $200,000, it is also subject to Additional Medicare Tax withholding. However, when group-term life insurance over $50,000 is provided to an employee (including retirees) after his or her termination, the employee share of social security and Medicare taxes and Additional Medicare Tax on that period of coverage is paid by the former employee with his or her tax return and is not collected by the employer. In this case, an employer should report this income as wages on Form 941, Employer's QUARTERLY Federal Tax Return (or the employer's applicable employment tax return), and make a current period adjustment to reflect any uncollected employee social security, Medicare, or Additional Medicare Tax on group-term life insurance. However, unlike the uncollected portion of the regular (1.45%) Medicare tax, an employer may not report the uncollected Additional Medicare Tax in box 12 of Form W-2 with code N.

34. **For employees who receive third-party sick pay, will wages paid by an employer and by the third party need to be aggregated to determine whether the $200,000 withholding threshold has been met?**

Yes. Wages paid by an employer and by the third party need to be aggregated to determine whether the $200,000 withholding threshold has been met. The same rules that currently assign responsibility for sick pay reporting and payment of Medicare tax based on which party is treated as the employer (that is, the employer, the employer's agent, or a third party that is not the employer's agent) apply also to Additional Medicare Tax. For more information on sick pay, see Publication 15-A, Employer's Supplemental Tax Guide, and Notice 91-26, 1991-2 C.B. 619.

35. **If an employee has amounts deferred under a nonqualified deferred compensation (NQDC) plan, when is the nonqualified deferred compensation taken into account as wages for purposes of withholding Additional Medicare Tax?**

An employer calculates wages for purposes of withholding Additional Medicare Tax from nonqualified deferred compensation (NQDC) in the same way that it calculates wages for withholding the existing Medicare tax from NQDC. Thus, if an employee has amounts deferred under a nonqualified deferred compensation plan and the NQDC is taken into account as wages for FICA tax purposes under the special timing

124

rule described in §31.3121(v)(2)-1(a)(2) of the Employment Tax Regulations, the NQDC would likewise be taken into account under the special timing rule for purposes of determining an employer's obligation to withhold Additional Medicare Tax. Additional information about the special timing rules for NQDC is in Publication 957, Reporting Back Pay and Special Wage Payments to the Social Security Administration.

36. **For a company that goes through a merger or acquisition, will the wages from the predecessor and successor employers be combined to determine whether the $200,000 withholding threshold has been met?**

When corporate acquisitions meet certain requirements, wages paid by the predecessor are treated as if paid by the successor for purposes of applying the social security wage base and for applying the Additional Medicare Tax withholding threshold (that is, $200,000 in a calendar year).

37. **Should an employer combine an employee's wages for services performed for all of its subsidiaries if it has an employee who performs services for more than one subsidiary in its company, but the payroll is paid through one of the subsidiaries?**

An employer is required to withhold Additional Medicare Tax on wages paid to an employee in excess of $200,000 in a calendar year. When an employee is performing services for multiple subsidiaries of a company, and each subsidiary is an employer of the employee with regard to the services the employee performs for that subsidiary, the wages paid by the payor on behalf of each subsidiary should be combined only if the payor is a common paymaster. Publication 15-A, section 7 contains more information on common paymasters. The wages are not combined for purposes of the $200,000 withholding threshold if the payor is not a common paymaster.

38. **I am a common paymaster that pays wages to an employee who is concurrently employed by related corporations. Should I combine this employee's wages for purposes of determining whether wages are paid in excess of the $200,000 withholding threshold?**

Yes. Liability to withhold Additional Medicare Tax with respect to wages disbursed by the common paymaster is computed as if there was a single employer, just as it is for application of the social security wage base. See section 7 of Publication 15-A for more information on common paymasters.

39. **If an agent pays wages to an employee on behalf of an employer (under an approved Form 2678, Employer Appointment of Agent), then, for purposes of determining whether wages are paid in excess of the $200,000 withholding threshold, should the agent combine those wages with wages paid to that same employee**

- **directly by the employer,**
- **by the same agent on behalf of a different employer, or**
- **by another agent on behalf of the same employer?**

No. Wages paid by an agent with an approved Form 2678 on behalf of an employer should not be combined with wages paid to the same employee by any of the above other parties in determining whether to withhold Additional Medicare Tax.

40. **I use an employee leasing company. How should wages be determined for purposes of the $200,000 withholding threshold?**

An employer is required to withhold Additional Medicare Tax on wages paid to an employee in excess of $200,000 in a calendar year. Generally, if you provide wages in excess of the $200,000 withholding threshold to the employee leasing company to pay to an employee that performs services for you, Additional Medicare Tax should be withheld from the wages in excess of $200,000. Taxpayers should be aware that the employer is ultimately responsible for the deposit and payment of federal tax liabilities. Even though you forward tax payments to a third party to make the tax deposits, you may be responsible as the employer for the tax liability.

41. **Will the IRS be changing Form 941 or any other forms for tax year 2013 to be completed by employers and payroll service providers?**

Yes. For example, a line will be added to Form 941 on which employers will report any individual's wages paid during the quarter that is in excess of $200,000 for the year, and on which employers will report their withholding liability for Additional

Medicare Tax on those wages. The existing line, on which employers report the liability for regular Medicare tax on all wages, will remain unchanged.

However, there will be no change to Form W-2. Additional Medicare Tax withholding on wages subject to Federal Insurance Contributions Act (FICA) taxes will be reported in combination with withholding of regular Medicare tax in box 6 ("Medicare tax withheld").

The IRS plans to release drafts of revised forms, including Forms 941, 943, and the tax return schemas for the F94X series of returns.

42. **When an employer deposits Additional Medicare Tax through the Electronic Federal Tax Payment System (EFTPS), does it need to separate Additional Medicare Tax from regular Medicare tax?**

No. When providing the deposit detail, regular Medicare tax and Additional Medicare Tax are entered as one combined amount.

43. **If an employer underwithholds Additional Medicare Tax (for example, fails to withhold the tax when it pays the employee wages in excess of $200,000 in a calendar year) and discovers the error in the same year the wages are paid but after its Form 941 is filed, how can the employer correct this error?**

An employer is liable for Additional Medicare Tax required to be withheld, whether or not it deducts the tax from wages it pays to the employee. If the employer fails to withhold the correct amount of Additional Medicare Tax from wages it pays to an employee and discovers the error in the same year it pays the wages, the employer may correct the error by making an interest-free adjustment on the appropriate corrected return (for example, Form 941-X). Once the employer has discovered the error, the employer should deduct the correct amount of Additional Medicare Tax from other wages or other remuneration, if any, it pays to the employee on or before the last day of the calendar year. However, even if the employer is not able to deduct the correct amount of Additional Medicare Tax from other wages or other remuneration it pays to the employee, the employer must report and pay the correct amount of Additional Medicare Tax on its return. If the employer pays Additional Medicare Tax without having deducted it from wages or other remuneration it pays to the employee, the obligation of the employee to the employer with respect to the payment is a matter for settlement between the employer and the employee.

44. **If an employer overwithholds Additional Medicare Tax (for example, withholds the tax before it pays the employee wages in excess of $200,000 in a calendar year) and discovers the error in the same year the wages are paid, how can the employer correct this error?**

The employer may correct the error by making an interest-free adjustment on the appropriate corrected return (for example, Form 941-X). The employer must first repay or reimburse the overwithheld amount to the employee prior to the end of the calendar year in which it paid the wages. If the employer does not repay or reimburse the employee the amount of overcollected Additional Medicare Tax before the end of the year in which the wages were paid, the employer should not correct the error via an interest-free adjustment. In this case, the employer should report the amount of withheld Additional Medicare Tax on the employee's Form W-2 so that the employee may obtain credit for Additional Medicare Tax withheld on the employee's individual income tax return.

45. **If an employer overwithholds Additional Medicare Tax (for example, withholds the tax before it pays the employee wages in excess of $200,000 in a calendar year) from an employee's wages, should the employer file a claim for refund for the Additional Medicare Tax?**

No. An employer should only claim a refund of overpaid Additional Medicare Tax if it did not deduct or withhold the overpaid Additional Medicare Tax from the employee's wages. The employer should correct the error by making an interest-free adjustment on the appropriate corrected return (for example, Form 941-X).

46. **If an employer underwithholds Additional Medicare Tax (for example, fails to withhold the tax when it pays the employee wages in excess of $200,000 in a calendar year) and discovers the error in a subsequent year, should the employer correct this error by making an interest-free adjustment?**

No. If an employer underwithholds Additional Medicare Tax and does not discover the error in the same year wages were paid, the employer should not correct the error by making an interest-free adjustment. However, to the extent the employer can show that the employee paid Additional Medicare Tax, the underwithheld amount will not be collected from the employer. The employer will remain subject to any applicable penalties.

47. **If an employer overwithholds Additional Medicare Tax (for example, withholds the tax before it pays the employee wages in excess of $200,000 in a calendar year) and discovers the error in a subsequent year, should the employer correct this error by making an interest-free adjustment?**

No. If an employer withholds more than the correct amount of Additional Medicare Tax from wages paid to an employee and does not discover the error in the same year the wages were paid, the employer should not correct the error by making an interest-free adjustment. In this case, the employer should report the amount of withheld Additional Medicare Tax on the employee's Form W-2 so that the employee may obtain credit for Additional Medicare Tax withheld. Additional Medicare Tax withholding will be applied against the taxes shown on the employee's individual income tax return (Form 1040).

Small Business Health Care Tax Credit

This new credit helps small businesses and small tax-exempt organizations afford the cost of covering their employees and are specifically targeted for those with low- and moderate-income workers. The credit is designed to encourage small employers to offer health insurance coverage for the first time or maintain coverage they already have. In general, the credit is available to small employers that pay at least half the cost of single coverage for their employees.

How will the credit make a difference for you?

For tax years 2010 through 2013, the maximum credit is 35 percent for small business employers and 25 percent for small tax-exempt employers such as charities. An enhanced version of the credit will be effective beginning Jan. 1, 2014. Additional information about the enhanced version will be added to IRS.gov as it becomes available. In general, on Jan. 1, 2014, the rate will increase to 50 percent and 35 percent, respectively.

Here's what this means for you. If you pay $50,000 a year toward workers' health care premiums – and if you qualify for a 15 percent credit, you save ... $7,500. If you save $7,500 a year from tax year 2010 through 2013, that's total savings of $30,000. If, in 2014, you qualify for a slightly larger credit, say 20 percent, your savings go from $7,500 a year to $12,000 a year.

Even if you are a small business employer who did not owe tax during the year, you can carry the credit back or forward to other tax years. Also, since the amount of the health insurance premium payments are more than the total credit, eligible small businesses can still claim a business expense deduction for the premiums in excess of the credit. That's both a credit and a deduction for employee premium payments.

There is good news for small tax-exempt employers too. The credit is refundable, so even if you have no taxable income, you may be eligible to receive the credit as a refund so long as it does not exceed your income tax withholding and Medicare tax liability.

And finally, if you can benefit from the credit this year but forgot to claim it on your tax return there's still time to file an amended return.

Can you claim the credit?

Now that you know how the credit can make a difference for your business, let's determine if you can claim it.

To be eligible, you must cover at least 50 percent of the cost of single (not family) health care coverage for each of your employees. You must also have fewer than 25 full-time equivalent employees (FTEs). Those employees must have average wages of less than $50,000 a year.

Let us break it down for you even more.

You are probably wondering: what *IS* a full-time equivalent employee. Basically, two half-time workers count as one full-timer. Here is an example, 20 half-time employees are equivalent to 10 full-time workers. That makes the number of FTEs 10 not 20.

Now let's talk about average wages. Say you pay total wages of $200,000 and have 10 FTEs. To figure average wages you divide $200,000 by 10 – the number of FTEs – and the result is your average wage. The average wage would be $20,000.

Also, the amount of the credit you receive works on a sliding scale. The smaller the business or charity, the bigger the credit. So if you have more than 10 FTEs or if the average wage is more than $25,000, the amount of the credit you receive will be less.

How do you claim the credit?

You must use Form 8941, Credit for Small Employer Health Insurance Premiums, to calculate the credit. If you are a small business, include the amount as part of the general business credit on your income tax return.

If you are a tax-exempt organization, include the amount on line 44f of the Form 990-T, Exempt Organization Business Income Tax Return. You must file the Form 990-T in order to claim the credit, even if you don't ordinarily do so. Don't forget ... if you are a small business employer you may be able to carry the credit back or forward. And if you are a tax-exempt employer, you may be eligible for a refundable credit

Health Insurance Premium Tax Credit

Starting in 2014, individuals and families can take a new premium tax credit to help them afford health insurance coverage purchased through an Affordable Insurance Exchange. Exchanges will operate in every state and the District of Columbia. The premium tax credit is refundable so taxpayers who have little or no income tax liability can still benefit. The credit also can be paid in advance to a taxpayer's insurance company to help cover the cost of premiums.

The proposed regulations provided that, for taxable years beginning before January 1, 2015, an eligible employer-sponsored plan is affordable for related individuals if the portion of the annual premium the employee must pay for self-only coverage (the required contribution percentage) does not exceed 9.5% of the taxpayer's household income. While several comments supported this rule, other comments asserted that the affordability of coverage for related individuals should be based on the portion of the annual premium the employee must pay for family coverage.

These final regulations adopt the proposed rule without change. The language of section 36B, through a cross-reference to section 5000A (e)(1)(B), specifies that the affordability test for

131

related individuals is based on the cost of self-only coverage. By contrast, section 5000A, which establishes the shared responsibility payment applicable to individuals for failure to maintain minimum essential coverage, addresses affordability for employees in section 5000A(e)(1)(B) and, separately, for related individuals in section 5000A(e)(1)(C). Thus, proposed regulations under section 5000A, which the Treasury Department is releasing concurrently with these final regulations, provide that, for purposes of applying the affordability exemption from the shared responsibility payment in the case of related individuals, the required contribution is based on the premium the employee would pay for employer-sponsored family coverage.

Effective/Applicability Date

These final regulations apply to taxable years ending after December 31, 2013.

Employer Shared Responsibility Payment

Starting in 2014, certain employers must offer health coverage to their full-time employees or a shared responsibility payment may apply.

Basics of the Employer Shared Responsibility Provisions

1. What are the Employer Shared Responsibility provisions?

Starting in 2014, employers employing at least a certain number of employees (generally 50 full-time employees and full-time equivalents, explained more fully below) will be subject to the Employer Shared Responsibility provisions under section 4980H of the Internal Revenue Code (added to the Code by the Affordable Care Act). Under these provisions, if these employers do not offer affordable health coverage that provides a minimum level of coverage to their full-time employees, they may be subject to an Employer Shared Responsibility payment if at least one of their full-time employees receives a premium tax credit for purchasing individual coverage on one of the new Affordable Insurance Exchanges.

To be subject to these Employer Shared Responsibility provisions, an employer must have at least 50 full-time employees or a combination of full-time and part-time employees that is equivalent to at least 50 full-time employees (for example, 100 half-time employees equals

50 full-time employees). As defined by the statute, a full-time employee is an individual employed on average at least **30** hours per week (so half-time would be 15 hours per week).

2. When do the Employer Shared Responsibility provisions go into effect?

The Employer Shared Responsibility provisions generally go into effect on January 1, 2014. Employers will use information about the employees they employ during 2013 to determine whether they employ enough employees to be subject to these new provisions in 2014. See question 4 for more information on determining whether an employer is subject to the Employer Shared Responsibility provisions.

3. Is more detailed information available about the Employer Shared Responsibility provisions?

Yes. Treasury and the IRS have proposed regulations on the new Employer Shared Responsibility provisions. Comments on the proposed regulations may be submitted by mail, electronically, or hand-delivered, and are due by March 18, 2013.

Which Employers are Subject to the Employer Shared Responsibility provisions?

4. I understand that the employer shared responsibility provisions apply only to employers employing at least a certain number of employees? How does an employer know whether it employs enough employees to be subject to the provisions?

To be subject to the Employer Shared Responsibility provisions, an employer must employ at least 50 full-time employees or a combination of full-time and part-time employees that equals at least 50 (for example, 40 full-time employees employed 30 or more hours per week on average plus 20 half-time employees employed 15 hours per week on average are equivalent to 50 full-time employees). Employers will determine each year, based on their current number of employees, whether they will be considered a large employer for the next year. For example, if an employer has at least 50 full-time employees, (including full-time equivalents) for 2013, it will be considered a large employer for 2014.

Employers average their number of employees across the months in the year to see whether they meet the large employer threshold. The averaging can take account of fluctuations that many employers may experience in their work force across the year. For those employers that may be close to the 50 full-time employee (or equivalents) threshold and need to know what to do for 2014, special transition relief is available to help them count their employees in 2013. See question 19 below for information about this transition relief. The proposed regulations provide additional information about how to determine the average number of employees for a year, including information about how to take account of salaried employees who may not clock their hours and a special rule for seasonal workers.

5. If two or more companies have a common owner or are otherwise related, are they combined for purposes of determining whether they employ enough employees to be subject to the Employer Shared Responsibility provisions?

Yes, consistent with longstanding standards that apply for other tax and employee benefit purposes, companies that have a common owner or are otherwise related generally are combined together for purposes of determining whether or not they employ at least 50 full-time employees (or an equivalent combination of full-time and part-time employees). If the combined total meets the threshold, then each separate company is subject to the Employer Shared Responsibility provisions, even those companies that individually do not employ enough employees to meet the threshold. (The rules for combining related employers do not apply for purposes of determining whether an employer owes an Employer Shared Responsibility payment or the amount of any payment). The proposed regulations provide information on the rules for determining whether companies are related and how they are applied for purposes of the Employer Shared Responsibility provisions.

6. Do the Employer Shared Responsibility provisions apply only to large employers that are for-profit businesses or to other large employers as well?

All employers that employ at least 50 full-time employees or an equivalent combination of full-time and part-time employees are subject to the Employer Shared Responsibility provisions, including for-profit, non-profit and government entity employers.

7. Which employers are not subject to the Employer Shared Responsibility provisions?

Employers who employ fewer than 50 full-time employees (or the equivalent combination of full-time and part-time employees) are not subject to the Employer Shared Responsibility provisions. An employer with at least 50 full-time employees (or equivalents) will not be subject to an Employer Shared Responsibility payment if the employer offers affordable health coverage that provides a minimum level of coverage to its full-time employees.

8. Are companies with employees working outside the United States subject to the Employer Shared Responsibility provisions?

For purposes of determining whether an employer meets the 50 full-time employee (or full-time employees and full-time employee equivalents) threshold, an employer generally will take into account only work performed in the United States. For example, if a foreign employer has a large workforce worldwide, but less than 50 full-time (or equivalent) employees in the United States, the foreign employer generally would not be subject to the Employer Shared Responsibility provisions.

9. Are companies that employ US citizens working abroad subject to the Employer Shared Responsibility provisions?

A company that employs U.S. citizens working abroad generally would be subject to the Employer Shared Responsibility provisions only if the company had at least 50 full-time employees (or the equivalent combination of full-time and part-time employees), determined by taking into account only work performed in the United States. Accordingly, employees working only abroad, whether or not U.S. citizens, generally will not be taken into account for purposes of determining whether an employer meets the 50 full-time employee (or equivalents) threshold. Furthermore, for employees working abroad the time spent working for the employer outside of the U.S. would not be taken into account for purposes of determining whether the employer owes an Employer Shared Responsibility payment or the amount of any such payment.

Liability for the Employer Shared Responsibility Payment

10. Under what circumstances will an employer owe an Employer Shared Responsibility payment?

In 2014, if an employer meets the 50 full-time employee threshold, the employer generally will be liable for an Employer Shared Responsibility payment only if:

(a) The employer does not offer health coverage or offers coverage to less than 95% of its full-time employees, and at least one of the full-time employees receives a premium tax credit to help pay for coverage on an Exchange;

OR

(b) The employer offers health coverage to at least 95% of its full-time employees, but at least one full-time employee receives a premium tax credit to help pay for coverage on an Exchange, which may occur because the employer did not offer coverage to that employee or because the coverage the employer offered that employee was either unaffordable to the employee (see question 11, below) or did not provide minimum value (see question 12, below).

After 2014, the rule in paragraph (a) applies to employers that do not offer health coverage or that offer coverage to less than 95% of their full time employees and the dependents of those employees.

11. How does an employer know whether the coverage it offers is affordable?

If an employee's share of the premium for employer-provided coverage would cost the employee more than 9.5% of that employee's annual household income, the coverage is not considered affordable for that employee. If an employer offers multiple healthcare coverage options, the affordability test applies to the lowest-cost option available to the employee that also meets the minimum value requirement (see question 12, below.)

Because employers generally will not know their employees' household incomes, employers can take advantage of one of the affordability safe harbors set forth in the proposed regulations. Under the safe harbors, an employer can avoid a payment if the cost of the coverage to the employee would not exceed 9.5% of the wages the employer pays the employee that year, as reported in Box 1 of Form W-2, or if the coverage satisfies either of two other design-based affordability safe harbors.

12. How does an employer know whether the coverage it offers provides minimum value?

A minimum value calculator will be made available by the IRS and the Department of Health and Human Services (HHS). The minimum value calculator will work in a similar fashion to the actuarial value calculator that HHS is making available. Employers can input certain information about the plan, such as deductibles and co-pays, into the calculator and get a determination as to whether the plan provides minimum value by covering at least 60 percent of the total allowed cost of benefits that are expected to be incurred under the plan.

13. If an employer wants to be sure it is offering coverage to all of its full-time employees, how does it know which employees are full-time employees? Does the employer need to offer the coverage to all of its employees because it won't know for certain whether an employee is a full-time employee for a given month until after the month is over and the work has been done?

The proposed regulations provide a method to employers for determining in advance whether or not an employee is to be treated as a full-time employee, based on the hours of service credited to the employee during a previous period. Using this look-back method to measure hours of service, the employer will know the employee's status as a full-time employee at the time the employer would offer coverage. The proposed regulations are consistent with IRS notices that have previously been issued and describe approaches that can be used for various circumstances, such as for employees who work variable hour schedules, seasonal employees, and teachers who have time off between school years.

Calculation of the Employer Shared Responsibility Payment

14. If an employer that does not offer coverage or offers coverage to less than 95% of its employees owes an Employer Shared Responsibility payment, how is the amount of the payment calculated?

In 2014, if an employer employs enough employees to be subject to the Employer Shared Responsibility provisions and does not offer coverage during the calendar year to at least

95% of its full-time employees, it owes an Employer Shared Responsibility payment equal to the number of full-time employees the employer employed for the year (minus 30) multiplied by $2,000, as long as at least one full-time employee receives the premium tax credit. (Note that for purposes of this calculation, a full-time employee does not include a full-time equivalent). For an employer that offers coverage for some months but not others during the calendar year, the payment is computed separately for each month for which coverage was not offered. The amount of the payment for the month equals the number of full-time employees the employer employed for the month (minus up to 30) multiplied by 1/12 of $2,000. If the employer is related to other employers (see question 5 above), then the 30-employee exclusion is allocated among all the related employers. The payment for the calendar year is the sum of the monthly payments computed for each month for which coverage was not offered. After 2014, these rules apply to employers that do not offer coverage or that offer coverage to less than 95% of their full time employees and the dependents of those employees.

15. If an employer offers coverage to at least 95% of its employees, and, nevertheless, owes the Employer Shared Responsibility payment, how is the amount of the payment calculated?

For an employer that offers coverage to at least 95% of its full-time employees in 2014, but has one or more full-time employees who receive a premium tax credit, the payment is computed separately for each month. The amount of the payment for the month equals the number of full-time employees who receive a premium tax credit for that month multiplied by 1/12 of $3,000. The amount of the payment for any calendar month is capped at the number of the employer's full-time employees for the month (minus up to 30) multiplied by 1/12 of $2,000. (The cap ensures that the payment for an employer that offers coverage can never exceed the payment that employer would owe if it did not offer coverage). After 2014, these rules apply to employers that offer coverage to at least 95% of full time employees and the dependents of those employees.

Making an Employer Shared Responsibility Payment

16. How will an employer know that it owes an Employer Shared Responsibility payment?

The IRS will contact employers to inform them of their potential liability and provide them an opportunity to respond before any liability is assessed or notice and demand for payment is made. The contact for a given calendar year will not occur until after employees' individual tax returns are due for that year claiming premium tax credits and after the due date for employers that meet the 50 full-time employee (plus full-time equivalents) threshold to file the information returns identifying their full-time employees and describing the coverage that was offered (if any).

17. How will an employer make an Employer Shared Responsibility payment?

If it is determined that an employer is liable for an Employer Shared Responsibility payment after the employer has responded to the initial IRS contact, the IRS will send a notice and demand for payment. That notice will instruct the employer on how to make the payment. Employers will not be required to include the Employer Shared Responsibility payment on any tax return that they file.

Transition Relief

18. I understand that the Employer Shared Responsibility provisions do not go into effect until 2014. However, the health plan that I offer to my employees runs on a fiscal plan year that starts in 2013 and will run into 2014. Do I need to make sure my plan complies with these new requirements in 2013 when the next fiscal plan year starts?

For an employer that as of December 27, 2012, already offers health coverage through a plan that operates on a fiscal year (a fiscal year plan), transition relief is available. First, for any employees who are eligible to participate in the plan under its terms as of December 27, 2012 (whether or not they take the coverage), the employer will not be subject to a potential payment until the first day of the fiscal plan year starting in 2014. Second, if (a) the fiscal year plan (including any other fiscal year plans that have the same plan year) was offered to at least one third of the employer's employees (full-time and part-time) at the most recent open season or (b) the fiscal year plan covered at least one quarter of the employer's employees, then the employer also will not be subject to the Employer Shared Responsibility payment with respect to any of its full-time employees until the first day of the fiscal plan year starting in 2014, provided that those full-time employees are offered affordable coverage that provides minimum value no later than that first day. So, for example, if during the most recent open season preceding December 27, 2012, an employer offered coverage under a fiscal year plan with a plan year starting on July 1, 2013 to at least one third of its employees (meeting the threshold for the additional relief), the employer could avoid liability for a payment if, by July 1, 2014, it expanded the plan to offer coverage satisfying the Employer Shared Responsibility provisions to the full-time employees who had not been offered coverage. For purposes of determining whether the plan covers at least one quarter of the employer's employees, an employer may look at any day between October 31, 2012 and December 27, 2012.

19. Is transition relief available to help employers that are close to the 50 full-time employee threshold determine their options for 2014?

Yes. Rather than being required to use the full twelve months of 2013 to measure whether it has 50 full-time employees (or an equivalent number of part-time and full-time employees), an employer may measure using any six-consecutive-month period in 2013. So, for example, an employer could use the period from January 1, 2013, through June 30, 2013, and then have six months to analyze the results, determine whether it needs to offer a plan, and, if so, choose and establish a plan.

Additional Information

20. When can an employee receive a premium tax credit?

Premium tax credits generally are available to help pay for coverage for employees who

- are between 100% and 400% of the federal poverty level and enroll in coverage through an Affordable Insurance Exchange,
- are not eligible for coverage through a government-sponsored program like Medicaid or CHIP, and
- are not eligible for coverage offered by an employer or are eligible only for employer coverage that is unaffordable or that does not provide minimum value.

21. If an employer does not employ enough employees to be subject to the Employer Shared Responsibility provisions, does that affect the employer's employees' eligibility for a premium tax credit?

No. The rules for how eligibility for employer-sponsored insurance affects eligibility for the premium tax credit are the same, regardless of whether the employer employs enough employees to be subject to the Employer Shared Responsibility provisions.

22. Where can employees get more information about Affordable Insurance Exchanges?

The Department of Health and Human Services is developing the rules for exchanges.

23. The Treasury Department and the IRS have proposed regulations on the Employer Shared Responsibility provisions that are proposed to be effective for months after December 31, 2013. However, there are certain decisions and actions employers may have to take during 2013 to prepare for 2014. May employers rely on the proposed regulations during 2013 for guidance on the Employer Shared Responsibility provisions?

Yes. Taxpayers may rely on the proposed regulations for purposes of compliance with the Employer Shared Responsibility provisions. If the final regulations are more restrictive than the guidance in the proposed regulations, the final regulations will be applied prospectively, and employers will be given sufficient time to come into compliance with the final regulations.

Source:

http://www.irs.gov/uac/Affordable-Care-Act-Tax-Provisions

CHAPTER TEN

Beating Obamacare

Whether you're a perfectly healthy college student or someone struggling with a chronic disease, The Affordable Care Act—will likely affect you in some way.

The legislation, upheld by U.S. Supreme Court in June 2012, aims to shrink the number of uninsured Americans. But do you know how to take advantage of new opportunities for coverage form this legislation that is aims to shrink the number of uninsured Americans? Probably the biggest concern might be how will I be able to find a policy I can afford?

Below are various low cost health insurance options out there that, in fact, many Americans have already implemented and are beating the rising battle against being uninsured according to David Gibberman:

If you're like most people, you'll be able to qualify for generous subsidies from the federal government to purchase health insurance. The federal government will pay up to 100% of the cost of health insurance for individuals whose household income does not exceed four times the federal poverty level. Last year, four times the federal poverty level was $44,680 for an individual and $92,200 ($115,280 in Alaska) for a family of four.

If your household income is too high to make you eligible for Medicaid but too low to make you eligible for federal subsidies to purchase health insurance, either try to get another job or reduce your income. Under Obamacare, the federal government will help people purchase health insurance only if their household income is at least 100% of the poverty level for a family of their size. Those with less income will have to do without health insurance if their state Medicaid program doesn't cover them.

If you can qualify for premium assistance, don't get a job with an employer that offers

health insurance, particularly if you're married and/or have children. If you take a job with an employer that offers health insurance, you won't be eligible for federal premium assistance. Worse, employers have to offer health insurance that is affordable for individuals (i.e., costing no more than 9.5% of an individual's wages) but don't have to offer affordable coverage for families.

Live with the person you love; don't get married. If you live with someone, that person's income won't count when determining your eligibility for federal premium assistance. But it will count if you get married. For example, if your income is $44,000 and you're living with someone making $40,000, you each can qualify for federal premium assistance. But if you marry, neither of you can qualify for assistance. Several analysts point out that Obamacare develops a marriage penalty. Simply put, individuals lose subsidies if they choose to marry without any change to earnings. Representative Darrel Issa (R–CA) points out a simple explanation and example: "The result of linking the tax credit to the federal poverty level is that two individuals who make between $61,600 and $91,200 in 2014 will not benefit from the tax credit if they decide to marry."

While this example only shows one case, it is true that most individuals that previously obtained exchange subsidies would lose some subsidies when becoming married. For a couple that has two individual earners between 100 percent and 400 percent of the Federal Poverty Level, choosing to get married would experience further increases in effective marginal tax rates—between 10 percent and 24 percent.

Don't accept a raise until you've talked with your tax adviser. Before accepting a pay raise, make sure the added money won't disqualify you for federal premium assistance or reduce the amount of assistance by more than the amount of the raise. Whenever possible, get raises in the form of nontaxable compensation (such as employer contributions to a retirement or flexible spending plan or educational assistance).

If you have children who are dependents, keep close tabs on their summer earnings. Although it's generally not considered a good idea these days to have your children stand out from their peers by showing initiative and a work ethic, it's a particularly bad idea if you want the federal government to subsidize your health insurance. Money that dependents earn is added to your household income and can disqualify you for premium assistance. **If your state hasn't established an exchange to sell health insurance, consider moving to**

a state that has. Obamacare says it won't pay health insurance premiums for residents of states that haven't established an exchange. The Obama administration has said that it doesn't matter what the law actually says, but there's always a chance that the courts will enforce the law as written.

If it's going to cost you more for health insurance than the penalty for not purchasing a policy, skip the health insurance. After all, insurers will no longer be able to deny you coverage if you have a pre-existing condition. With careful planning, you can even avoid the penalty for not purchasing insurance. All you have to do is claim enough withholding allowances so that you're never owed a refund. Unlike other tax penalties, the IRS can't garnish your wages or seize any of your property to collect what you owe. It can only deduct the penalty from any refund you're due.

Nevertheless, it is not advisable to take advantage of other taxpayers by opting-out insurance until it is needed since the high cost of hospitalization and medical care means that lacking health insurance could put you and your family at risk of being one injury or diagnosis away from bankruptcy. Statistics show that lacking health insurance poses a greater risk of financial catastrophe than lacking car insurance or homeowner's insurance.

One of the primary purposes of health insurance is to protect against the risk of incurring unaffordable medical bills. Although people are 50-percent more likely to have car accident than to be hospitalized in a given year, the average bill for a hospital visit is over two and a half times higher than the average loss for a car accident. And, while the bill for a single hospitalization is about the same as the average loss from a house fire, a person is ten times more likely to be hospitalized than to experience a house fire.

Ultimately, uninsured families are forced to choose between going without care or facing health care bills they are unable to pay. When the uninsured receive care they cannot afford, other payers must absorb the cost. This uncompensated care leads to higher costs for Americans with insurance and their employers.

Having so many uninsured Americans is unsafe and unsustainable. Health insurance is crucial to protecting people from unexpected hospital costs. But what do you do when you don't have a job and can't get affordable individual or family health insurance from an employer? Or, what about all the families that have jobs but still cannot afford the health insurance offered by their employers and can't find an option for affordable health insurance? With the passage of the Affordable Care Act, families now have more freedom and control over their health care choices. From discounts and subsidies to specially designed plans for young adults, the heath-care law provides measures to help make insurance more affordable for people with low and moderate incomes.

If you don't qualify for Medicaid, you may also be eligible for a tax credit if your income is under 400% of the Federal poverty level (roughly under $43,000 for an individual, or $88,000 for a family of four). You get the tax credit each month, instead of waiting for you annual tax rebate. You also can get subsidies to lower out-of-pocket costs, such as deductibles and co-payments if you earn less than $34,516 for an individual or $70,275 for a family of four and purchase your policy on health insurance in the online marketplaces.

It is not easy for people without health insurance to receive adequate care. Instead, uninsured individuals must make the decision to receive life saving care now, only to be plagued with bankruptcy and financial ruin in the future. However, thanks to the reforms driven by the Affordable Care Act, more people will be able to receive comprehensive coverage and fewer will have to delay care.

Did you enjoy this book? Then you'll love---

No Easy Hunt: The First Definitive Account of the Rise and Fall of Osama bin laden [Kindle Edition]

Several memoirs, reminiscences, and commentaries about Bin laden have made their way into the public consciousness of the past decade, and yet there exist no biography that chronicles Bin Laden's life from birth to death. Perusal of these works shows that they usually seek to serve one of the three aims: to produce a portrait of Bin laden, to narrate the hunt for him, or examine the ideological and paramilitary strategies of Al-Qaeda in general or on some particular point. But to gain a balancing understanding of his background, the development of his ideas, formation of Al Qaeda and importantly why he believe what he does, one needs a biographical treatments that define all the three areas together, and no such book exists---- which has resulted in the emergence of conflicting versions of who Bin laden is and what his goals are over the years.

In NO EASY HUNT, Bartholomew Okonkwo sidesteps the usual dichotomy, presenting instead a careful and extensive integration of the three aims in the exploration of Bin laden's evolution from his Saudi childhood as the son of a remote but reveled and very wealthy contractor all the way to the premature obituaries that contributed to his tragic death in Abbottabad Pakistan to arrive at a fresh understanding of the man, uncovering the roots of some of the most important—and dynamic forces that helped him in luring the U.S. into a financially ruinous "war on terrorism": as well as an invaluable look at that war and how the United States very nearly lost it, and the eventual defeat of Bin laden.

CPSIA information can be obtained at www.ICGtesting.com
Printed in the USA
LVOW03s2134160514

386211LV00005B/42/P